CRITICAL SKILLS

FOR

SOLVING DESIGN

PROBLEMS

CRITICAL SKILLS FOR SOLVING DESIGN PROBLEMS

USEFUL TIPS FROM ARCHITECTS IN PRACTICE

images
Publishing

Published in Australia in 2021 by
The Images Publishing Group Pty Ltd
ABN 89 059 734 431

Offices

Melbourne
6 Bastow Place
Mulgrave, Victoria 3170
Australia
Tel: +61 3 9561 5544

New York
6 West 18th Street 4B
New York, NY 10011
United States
Tel: +1 212 645 1111

Shanghai
6F, Building C, 838 Guangji Road
Hongkou District, Shanghai 200434
China
Tel: +86 021 31260822

books@imagespublishing.com
www.imagespublishing.com

A catalogue record for this
book is available from the
National Library of Australia

Title: Critical Skills for Solving Design Problems: Useful Tips from Architects in Practice
Author: Paul Michael Davis (Foreword)
ISBN: 9781864708554

Printed by Everbest Printing Investment Limited, in Hong Kong/China

IMAGES has included on its website a page for special notices in relation to this and its other publications.
Please visit www.imagespublishing.com

Contents

Paul Michael Davis

Principal Architect
Paul Michael Davis Architects

Before establishing his own practice, Paul Michael Davis had worked several years in internationally renowned architecture firms in Los Angeles and New York. While working in Frank Gehry's Los Angeles office, Paul developed advanced architectural concepts on projects such as the Louis Vuitton Foundation museum in Paris. He has also been a member of the Interior Design faculty of Bellevue College.

Paul attended the University of Washington, earning two bachelor's degrees in 2000, and a Master of Architecture in 2003. Paul is a registered architect in Washington State and a LEED Accredited Professional.

Foreword

How does an architect solve a design problem? Some architects can probably find the right solution on the first try. I am not one of them. Neither is Frank Gehry, whom I worked for at the beginning of my career.

Neither, it seems, is OMA, Jeanne Gang, Morphosis, or a host of others in the canon of remarkable contemporary architects. Rather, these designers seem content to go back to the drawing board as many times as it takes to get the design right. And it usually takes a lot of tries.

Consider this recollection by Zaha Hadid on the process of designing a table for an apartment renovation project in 1985: "We made models. [We] did some sketches and someone in the office made models. Everything was adjusted. The dining room table went through many sessions. First it was done very crudely, then I sketched it, then it changed again."[1] The final design for this project at 24 Cathcart Road is iconic, and the journey to get to this architectural achievement was by no means linear.

These legendary architects were trained, like most of us, at schools that operate on a critical model. Design students are given problems to solve—an imaginary site, a program and/or client, and perhaps some other parameters. Then, they spend weeks or months developing and refining a solution to that problem, their process punctuated by input from critics—their primary instructor at regular intervals and also typically, a jury of invited professionals and academics at pivotal or conclusive stages. A design that is universally loved by a jury will surely earn a high grade. With that said, no design proposal escapes without

1 Detlef Martins, Patrik Schumacher, Joseph Giovannini, and Zaha Hadid, *Zaha Hadid* (New York: Guggenheim Museum Publications, 2006), 49.

criticism; a strong academic critique can be one of the most energizing and inspiring moments of an architect's education, because in that instant of receiving and internalizing criticism, the designer grows. They see how their work falls short through the eyes of someone else—someone more trained and experienced in the subject they chose to study—and they see other possible solutions to the problem in that understanding.

A good design critic doesn't design a student's project for them. They listen to what the student is trying to do and tells them how and where their design is working against that end. As a result, when the student receives thoughtful critique, it is rewarding, rather than degrading. The critic becomes, briefly, a member of the student's design team, helping them to refine their ideas.

When the designer graduates from school, however, they (usually) land in a professional setting that has a very different attitude toward criticism and design. Client demands—often irrational—and code requirements—often stifling—become the main aspects that drive the design process and efficiency in creating a design becomes a priority consideration. Real projects have real consequences. Finances, life-safety responsibilities, deadlines, and political realities complicate the previously tidy cycle of "design, critique, revise."

Somewhere in that short time that the architecture student turns into a professional architect, criticism becomes a bad thing that causes the designer to question their most basic abilities and it eventually becomes better to avoid mistakes, unfortunately, at the expense of innovation.

Even with their maturing experience and growing competence, the quest to find a unique, creative solution to a given problem is often lost because of an altered mindset: since a design solution worked previously on another site for another client, then why not apply that same solution again and again, especially if the alternative is to face the possibility of failure.

The best architects manage to crack the code and surpass the challenges. They design buildings that make their clients happy and enrich their lives, and they also satisfy building codes and create safe environments for their users. These buildings make their communities stronger and more resilient, and they are unique expressions of an idea—specific solutions to specific problems, which bring something new and meaningful into the world.

I don't believe that these great designers are especially worried about efficiency or making mistakes. They have managed to carry that academic attitude toward criticism into their professional work. Their offices are filled with models, sketches on trace paper, and hard drives that keep expanding with ideas that will probably never see the light of day.

Critical Skills for Solving Design Problems poses fifteen unique questions to a diverse group of architects, to be answered as it applies (or has applied) to their work and to their project featured in the book. These questions are in essence statements about typical practices within the industry, or sets of rules that are shaped as questions—some of them grandiose—that at their core ask how these architects followed those rules.

These fifteen questions serve to extract a critique's inherent value. They address a designer who is open-minded, but who ultimately sticks to their chosen design concept. They encourage responsiveness throughout the design process and call on the architect to remain alert and constantly true to their goals. They do not, however, encourage efficiency or the avoidance of mistakes.

One particularly provocative commandment—that is not to make any prejudgments—elicited some of the most powerful responses from each of the architects in this book. Evidently, there is a familiar passion among these practitioners to avoid the formulaic. I believe that is the route of most great designers.

Jacques Herzog of the storied Swiss architecture firm, Herzog & de Meuron was once asked whether he would return to a particular design his office had done for the Serpentine Pavilion. His response was, "As a project it is complete. As a concept, it, like many of our projects, is a work in progress."[2]

Another pronouncement this book makes is believing that the effective design measure is promising even if it cannot be implemented at present. I see a parallel between this and Herzog's statement. In a critical design process, ideas may lose their relevance, but nonetheless, maintain future application. Similarly, an overall concept can apply to a given design problem and site and yet, have a different life and expression on a later project with a different set of unique circumstances. The process of "critiquing and revising" will yield a different result with those different parameters.

2 A.J.P. Artemel, Russel LeStourgeon, and Violette de la Selle, "Interview with Jacques Herzog," *Perspecta 49: The Yale Architecture Journal* (Cambridge: The MIT Press, 2016), 170.

The designers in this book are also asked about teamwork and looking for problems that may have been overlooked. I think it would be hard to find a good architect who disagreed with the importance of this principle. It takes more than one person to make something as substantial and complex as a building, and everyone contributing to that project deserves to have their voice heard. Designers really do need to collaborate to solve problems. The second part of the question, which asks architects to look for problems, dovetails with another vital skill: finding critical problems and seeking out solutions. In both cases, the architect is someone who not only solves problems, but finds them as well. As such, they are tasked with doing more than creating one simple answer. Every angle of a building, every consultant meeting, every relevant building code, every tree, and almost everything on or off a site is an opportunity for design engagement. In a similar vein, Frank Gehry wrote:

> "We start with site models and block models that we use to explore program and function and volumes. I sketch it out, and once we know it'll function then . . . we build model after model after model. We agonize about every little part of it, and I stare for hours and then I move something just a little bit, and I stare some more, and then it slowly starts to take shape. And the clients are around for all of this. They're a part of it, so we do it all together."[3]

Trying to understand clients' intentions (or sometimes cryptic demands) can be challenging for architects. Ironically, these demands often beg for empathy, which is hardly a dry, contractual emotion. This dictates that architects need to really listen to a client and try to understand what their intentions mean, and the completed structure those intentions hope to result in; it is also, I think, fodder for further critical thinking. It asks them to think past the simple project brief and get at

---

3   Frank Gehry and Brooke Hodge, *FOG: Flowing in All Directions* (Los Angeles: Circa Publishing, 2003), inside cover.

the deeper motivations driving the person, community, or organization commissioning a building.

The Situationists, an international group of thinkers and artists active between the late 1950s and early 1970s, have enjoyed a great deal of popularity among architects recently, especially in academia. I believe this is, at least in part, because this group emphasized a mode of living and creating that encouraged wandering and embraced chance. This touched on familiar territory for designers who have been through the critique-based studio education process.

At the center of Situationist ideology was "derive" or "drift." Rather than navigate a place, especially a city, according to a linear route or map, a Situationist would travel an intentionally non-linear path. Sometimes, these trips would be expressly counter-logical, such as exploring a region in Germany with the help of a map of Paris. One prominent Situationist, the artist Constant Nieuwenhuys, stated:

> "The liberation of behavior requires a social space that is labyrinthine, but at the same time continually subject to modification. There will no longer be any chance of getting off track in the sense of getting lost, but rather in the more positive sense of finding previously unknown paths."[4]

This book makes it a point to ask architects how they stay curious in complex and disordered situations. This proposition emphasizes the heart of critical dialogue, and perhaps, even goes a step further into a Situationist-like notion of finding new truths in non-linear models. When one remains curious, one doesn't dig one's heels in on an idea for there

---

4 From the chapter "The Principle of Disorientation," in *Situationists: Art, Politics, Urbanism*, edited by Xavier Costa et al (Barcelona: ACTAR, 1996), 87.

may be a better solution out there. Or maybe, there could be a solution that is truly new and creative.

Somewhere in the chaos and disorder of a project with a frightfully demanding client, a recalcitrant building official, a suboptimal building site, or an unhelpful builder, lie opportunities to make the design better. The disorder and complexity test the design solution. The architects in this book remind us to be willing to adjust our designs to these shifting demands without giving up the fundamental concept; they can actually make the solution better by revealing elements of a design that are inessential or even contrary to the needs of the project. To push the logic into Situationist territory: there is more truth in the disorientation than the prescribed path.

Embracing critique shifts the spatial metaphor from regulating lines and grids to labyrinths of discovery. This method of thinking can also yield a type of built space that is more responsive and rewarding to its users, instead of merely encouraging an inspiring design solution. In his essay "Theory of the Derive," Guy Debord, a prominent Situationist stated, "within architecture itself, the taste for deriving tends to promote all sorts of new forms of labyrinths made possible by modern techniques of construction."[5] In these pages, we see examples of how a non-linear, critical process can create brilliant spaces that would not otherwise have been possible following a top-down, linear process.

The Situationists were not simply passive wanderers, they were simultaneously revolutionaries. However, their rebellious philosophy was

---

5 From the essay "Theory of the Derive," in *Theory of the Derive and other Situationist Writings on the City*, edited by Asger Jorn (Barcelona: ACTAR, 2000), 23.

rooted in problematic traditions of gender and economic inequality.[6] Still, what resonates with architects of their ideas is less the revolutionary than the familiar. When a traveler follows an unprescribed, meandering, or even insane path, they often find unexpected rewards. Similarly, when an architect opens themselves up to criticism, they might find an answer that was otherwise elusive.

When I was in elementary school, I had a math test that asked us to actually explain how we would solve a particular algebra problem, rather than simply provide a number. I had, at that time, recently been introduced to the concept of "guess and check." I put that down as my answer and failed the test. I managed to learn algebra, of course, and some slightly more advanced math after that. But the basic strategy of guessing and checking has stuck with me as a guiding principle in my career as an architect. The truth is, I don't know if a solution to a design problem will work until I see it. So, I sketch, build physical models, construct endless digital models, mock things up at full size, and walk through the building as it is actually being built, and even at that point, *still* make adjustments. I don't have a formula and I don't think I ever will. Luckily, I'm not a mathematician.

Paul Michael Davis
Seattle, Washington, United States

---

6 Mary McLeod, "Everyday and 'Other' Spaces," *Architecture and Feminism* (New York: Princeton
   Architectural Press, 1996), 16. Columbia GSAPP Professor Mary McLeod wrote at length on this issue:
   "The Situationists attacked both bourgeois art (high modernism) and earlier avant-gardist movement . . .
   But as much as those of their predecessors, their visions of pleasure are permeated with sexism, a sexism
   inextricably entwined with their revulsion from bourgeois family life."

Case studies

"Architecture is the shaping of space for humans. Movement in the space architects create is fundamental."

Paul Michael Davis

Paul Michael Davis attended the University of Washington, earning two bachelor's degrees in 2000 and a Master of Architecture in 2003. Davis is a registered architect in Washington State and a LEED Accredited Professional. Before establishing his eponymous studio, Davis gained several years of experience in internationally renowned architecture firms in Los Angeles and New York. He developed advanced architectural concepts on projects while working in Frank Gehry's Los Angeles office, including the Louis Vuitton Foundation museum in Paris. Davis has also been a member of the Interior Design faculty of Bellevue College.

PROJECT NAME---Whole Earth Montessori School
LOCATION---Bothell, Washington, United States
COMPLETED---2017
AREA---3,878 square feet (360 square meters)
DESIGN---Paul Michael Davis Architects
PHOTOGRAPHY---Dale Lang, Paul Michael Davis

Paul Michael Davis Architects (PMDA) designed an addition to a rural campus by merging the school's pedagogy with the surrounding natural environment. Inspired by the Trinomial Cube—a teaching tool used by staff at Whole Earth Montessori School—the addition showcases a holistic design that helps students to visually absorb the concepts they are being taught.

A Trinomial Cube is a three-dimensional puzzle made of twenty-seven wooden blocks. PMDA represented each of the twenty-seven blocks with a window; the primary colors on some of the glass panes and the yellow entry door also reflect the school's main colors.

The school building is located in a lush creek-side meadow and had to be built on an existing foundation from the 1970s because the site is classified as a critical habitat where no new development is allowed. PMDA treated the rectangular-shaped concrete foundation as an opportunity to build a very simple cubic volume layered with complexity in the window design. Windows are inserted at the corners of the building to dematerialize the simple massing and bring light in from all sides. The largest window is located on the northern façade where it receives passive light, yet won't add excessive heat gain or glare to the structure. The large windows bring in ample natural light throughout the day and allow the students to remain engaged with nature. Large overhangs project from the building to shade the windows, and staircases on the outside of the building maximize interior space, while remaining within the original specified footprint of the structure.

How do you resolve the unfavorable aspects of site conditions?

Our Whole Earth Montessori project had a very constrained site. The project was a replacement of an existing building located in a sensitive wetland area. City zoning rules dictated that we couldn't extend the footprint, and the height of our new building couldn't exceed the height of the building being replaced. As our client needed as much space as possible, creating an expressive volume with reduced mass wasn't an option. We elected to accept the site conditions as they were and design a simple box with a gently sloping roof. However, we escaped the trap of those conditions by developing a complex fenestration design that created a variety of phenomenological spaces within the overall box, and expressed a concept that was larger than the site constraints.

How do you put forward solutions comprehensively and objectively without any prejudgments?

Design is about problem solving. For us, the best way to solve the problem is to come up with multiple alternative solutions. We then pick our three favorite solutions and develop those into fully realized 3D models and presentations. In Whole Earth Montessori, we presented all three solutions to our client. Each option had its own strength, but it was clear to all of us which idea was the best.

How do you perceive the abstract architectural space?

Architecture is the shaping of space for humans. Movement in the space architects create is fundamental. We work with 3D software that give us a real-time image of movement in the space. More important is the designer's understanding of the project in 3D in their imagination, and their ability to move through that imaginary space at will. In our Whole Earth Montessori design, we thought carefully about the relationship between the interior space and the natural setting, and how we could capture views of the surrounding landscape and create relationships with the other buildings and landscaped spaces on the site. These relationships come to life with movement.

How do you coordinate the relationship between function, space, style, and circulation?

Architecture is not a static mass, or even a simple empty space. We make buildings to serve needs, and those needs come with complex requirements. In Whole Earth Montessori, there was a need for circulation in all directions and complete flexibility in the layout of tables, chairs, and other curriculum elements. Our solution was two stacked, open spaces with minimal encumbrances, and we focused our attention on refining the enclosing volume, instead of complex space planning.

Sections

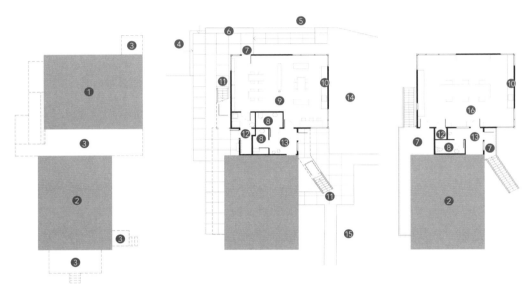

Floor plans

1 Phase 1: Replace 1970s house previously
   converted to classroom and offce
2 Phase 2: Replace 1970s garage previously
   converted into classroom and office
3 Decks, porches, and ramps removed
4 Drop-off/parking area
5 Driveway
6 Bench
7 Entry
8 Restroom
9 Classroom
10 Kitchen and storage
11 Stairs to upper level
12 Mechanical room
13 Lobby
14 Lawn
15 Play yard
16 Office/flexible space

How do your plans and ideas contribute in deriving a design?

We have found that diagramming is a very helpful activity throughout the design process. The diagram is a pure expression of the concept, and we like to check back in with our diagrams periodically in the development of our documents to make sure we are sticking to them. For this project, the diagram of the Trinomial Cube window blocks was really the most critical. Even while we were completing the final construction documents, we referred back to that diagram to make sure our final window dimensions were true to the proportions of the blocks.

How do you try to understand your clients' intentions?

Sometimes, artists will accept commissions from clients, but mostly, they create the work that they want to create, and if they are lucky, someone buys it. Architecture is almost always dependent on a client's commission, so understanding and meeting their intentions is the most fundamental task an architect carries out. In our case, we were fortunate to have a client who was passionate about design and who engaged in the process. There was a collaborative back-and-forth process with them and our design turned out better than it would have, had we been left to our own devices.

How do you incorporate your client's proposals into your design schemes?

Listen carefully to what your client is asking you to do. Then, find a creative way to solve their problems. In this project, our client was actively involved and we benefitted from their ideas in a design collaboration. It helps to admit that your client knows their project better than you do. They need your talent and design skills, but you need their knowledge. We had initially considered connecting the two floors of the Montessori school building in a number of ways, but our clients helped us understand how the two uses—an office space that can be flexibly used for older kids on the upper level, and a traditional classroom for younger kids—needed separation. That helped us clarify the project and focus on the Trinomial Cube window design as the real star of the design.

How do you make evaluations and judgments on your own schemes?

We look at multiple options whenever we are faced with a design problem. We do this at every scale of the design— from the overall site planning and concept design, down to the selection of door hardware. For us, having multiple options allows us to be critical and objectively decide which solution is actually the strongest.

How do you stay curious in complex and disordered situations?

There are opportunities for creative design expressions everywhere. The construction process of every building is complex and disordered, but we are always looking for ways to turn surprises in the construction process into unexpected meaningful features.

When designing, not all of an architect's ideas can always be fully realized. Could you share on how to handle such a situation?

We leave behind dozens, sometimes hundreds, of rejected design ideas on every project. We archive all of them and refer to them frequently. This tells us about our larger design process as a firm. But more importantly, it is a repository for ideas and solutions that could solve problems other than the ones they had originally intended to solve.

When you worked on this project, how did you strive to maintain your original idea from beginning to end?

We would prefer to say that the architect should not lose sight of the larger concept driving the project. It is often tempting to bring in a special material or a seductive space that has nothing to do with the overall design scheme. We have found that the final project is stronger if we resist this "collage" effect and stay focused on the direction we picked through our iterative process.

How do you make a comprehensive judgment on a design's progress and optimize the process?

We are always designing our design process, in a sense. We follow a trail forged by past successes, but every project is different. Therefore, a particular move, step, or rule that made sense in this design building might not make sense in the next.

How do you identify critical problems and seek solutions?

Our primary job as architects is to solve problems. However, we are often the ones to identify those problems in the first place. Our clients give us a list of needs, or "problems," but we are trained to think about space differently. It is important for us to identify the shortcomings of a site or project, or even our own design solution, and then propose a solution.

What role does teamwork play in identifying problems that may have been overlooked?

Buildings are far too big and complex for one person to claim all the credit. We are always, inevitably, working as a team. We troubleshoot our designs internally as a design team, but more importantly, we work closely with our clients and contractors to identify challenges to our design scheme and collaborate on creative solutions to those problems. During construction of the Montessori project, we went back and forth with our client and contractor to lay out the concrete steps, ramp, and bench at the front door. The end result is both a safety barrier blocking approaching cars, and a welcoming spot for kids to hang out. Our client and contractor deserve as much credit for the solution as we do.

How do you respond to unexpected problems that occur during the design process?

Don't forget that these unexpected problems are often opportunities to enrich your design and give your concept greater depth of meaning. In the case of our Montessori building, we had to contend with a complex fire sprinkler requirement that led to us designing a whole second phase for the project that wasn't originally planned. This was very rewarding because we had to duplicate our design of the flexible-use office space above a classroom on a different footprint on the north side of our original project. In the reinterpretation, we repeated the Trinomial Cube window concept as the driving design feature, but arranged the twenty-seven blocks in a different arrangement that responded to the different views, circulation, and configuration.

"A new project always benefits from the progress of a previous one."

Périphériques Architectes

Périphériques Architectes is a collective established by Emmanuelle Marin-Trottin and David Trottin of MARIN+TROTTIN Architectes. They often invite other architects to collaborate on ongoing projects and share opinions and ideas. Their work is backed by research and takes an experimental and multidisciplinary approach, incorporating architecture, urban planning, scenography, and communication. Périphériques' projects include residential, cultural, educational, and service facilities. The architects are particularly experienced in projects with programmatic complexities.

PROJECT NAME---Coallia Résidence and Restaurant Social
LOCATION---Paris, France
COMPLETED---2017
AREA---56,284 square feet (5,229 square meters)
DESIGN---Périphériques Architectes
PHOTOGRAPHY---Luc Boegly, Périphériques Architectes

Coallia Résidence and Restaurant Social is a new migrant workers home offering 173 studio-type houses and a restaurant. The design takes an environmental approach, working with parts of the existing buildings on the site, densifying the plot to protect a landscaped courtyard. One building has been preserved and restructured, while a second has been demolished to make way for a new construction.

The new buildings are unified with a homogenous façade of enamelled terra cotta cladding that reacts to the environment by emitting iridescent reflections of the sky and surrounding buildings.

The composition of the façade is designed around the windows (of which there are more than 350) of the173 studios, such that a repetitive pattern is avoided when viewed from the street. Three extruded terra cotta profiles were created with different surface angles and the iridescent enamel creates different visual and atmospheric effects when hit with light and reflections of the sky and surroundings.

There are colored sections on the first floor, which contains common areas, the laundry room, meeting rooms, offices, and a living room. These areas have glazing to allow light in and provide views. The restaurant has checkerboard-pattern floors and walls. The façade of the restaurant is marked by large black metal frames that evoke a basement effect. Each studio has a bathroom and kitchenette.

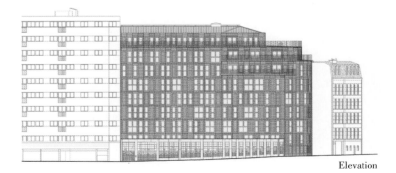

Elevation

How do you resolve the unfavorable aspects of site conditions?

The site rules and the condition of the existing building are fundamental when starting to reflect on the design. They are what's going to guide, nourish, and reveal our creative ideas for the design of the project.

After an accurate analysis of the multiple constraints of this new migrants home project, such as deadlines, phasing, environmental ambitions, amount of housing, and so on, we

decided to preserve part of the existing buildings, which are
two parallelepiped buildings set back from the street. They
were built in 1978 and designed by architect Anthony Bechu.
We chose to restructure and extend as the size of the existing
building allowed us to create more housing and enabled it
to be more energy efficient, compared to a demolition and
reconstruction. Moreover, the condition of the building structure
was compatible with the development of new housing types.

How do you put forward solutions comprehensively and objectively without any prejudgments?

Even though they are complex and difficult, our studies excite us and we never give up. It is the magical part of our profession. It is never the same, always different. Nothing can be predicted in advance because the contexts and parameters around each project are unique. It is an adventure; a new story every time.

How do you perceive the abstract architectural space?

Spatial visualization is always important in our work. We still work a lot with classical cardboard models—more than with digital ones—and at different scales. This allows us to visually browse the spaces and move around in, and through them.

How do you coordinate the relationship between function, space, style, and circulation?

The combination that results from the site conditions and the program is always unique and particular, and that is what makes a unique and dedicated project emerge.

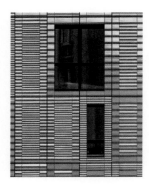

For the new migrants housing project, the choice was to work with the existing building, to dandify the plot, and to redefine the urban skyline of the building. Thus, we preserved and restructured the building, and demolished the second building to make way for a new construction along the streets to constitute a continuous urban front. This new density preserves a landscaped courtyard inside the plot. All of these constructions are unified, without distinction between rehabilitated parts and new parts, thanks to a homogenous façade design. The enamelled terra cotta cladding reacts to the environment by emitting iridescent reflections of the sky and surrounding buildings.

How do your plans and ideas contribute in deriving a design?

Our work is based on research. Every result, even partial, is part of our experiences and will be eventually reused and continued if the project is accepted. A new project always benefits from the progress of a previous one.

How do you try to understand your clients' intentions?

Our clients' intentions are of course the question that we have to answer, so we will do our best to satisfy them. But, as we take on the advisor position as architect and strengthen our proposal, the client will realize that their intentions are not always the best and ideal, so we can lead them to reconsider other solutions to solve the problem. These are new points of view that also allow clients to appropriate the project.

How do you incorporate your client's proposals into your design schemes?

You have to know how to nuance their purpose, to present alternatives, to discuss and be diplomatic, and whether or not to integrate the proposals.

How do you make evaluations and judgments on your own schemes?

The evaluation is often by the users of the building, as well as the inhabitants of the neighborhood who appreciate, comment, validate, and judge it. For Coallia housing, the existing building was very damaged and many people wished to see it removed. Now, people come to look at and touch the new building to appreciate its fascinating materiality.

How do you stay curious in complex and disordered situations?

We appreciate complex projects. The idea of finding order with a simple solution is a gratifying aspect of our work, even while having to fight with multiple data to achieve it. For Coallia, we had to arrange 173 studios on a very small plot while trying to offer a pleasant point of view for everyone.

When designing, not all of an architect's ideas can always be fully realized. Could you share on how to handle such a situation?

Our work is the result of constant research. Some research can be applied to ongoing projects, while others

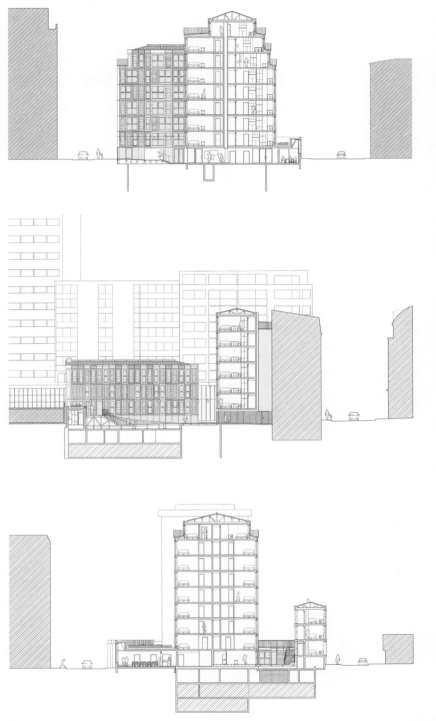

Sections

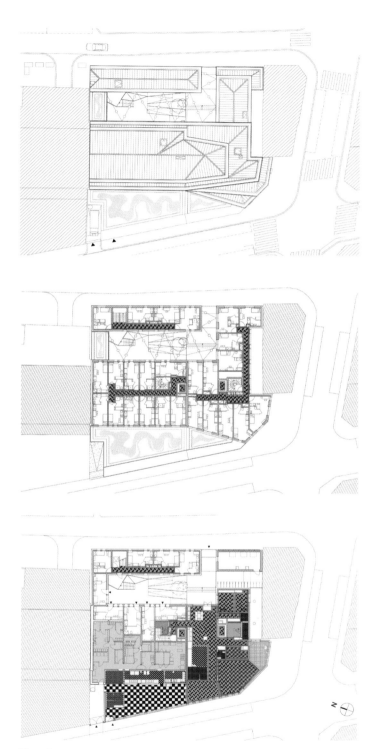

Floor plans

will be developed in the future. For twenty-five years now, we have been experimenting with material, seeking to give it form and a specific state to resolve the problem concerned. We try go a little further for each project. Our work is a perpetual progression.

When you worked on this project, how did you strive to maintain your original idea from beginning to end?

Sometimes the schemes that deviate are sources of new or different elements that come to feed the project. Previous research fulfills the reflection and enriches the development of the conception that generates new directions in the work.

How do you make a comprehensive judgment on a design's progress and optimize the process?

After twenty-five years of experience, our conceptions have become more mature and there is less wasted time in our research work. We know better what we do not want and what we have already tested. The work is quicker in a way.

How do you identify critical problems and seek solutions?

This is the heart of our work: to seek out solution. But also to innovate, propose, and invent new forms of space, of design, and of graphics. At multiple levels, we renew ourselves and find the right solutions.

What role does teamwork play in identifying problems that may have been overlooked?

It has been twenty-five years since we founded the Périphériques collective to develop more sharing and create exchanges and critical work meetings on each project, both at their conception and during the construction process. These exchanges are the DNA of our approach, even if nowadays we evolve more autonomously.

How do you respond to unexpected problems that occur during the design process?

Each project is different and has its share of unexpected problems. They are obviously never the same. This is part of our job and is always an intense challenge that motivates us to find the best solution to the problem that may arise.

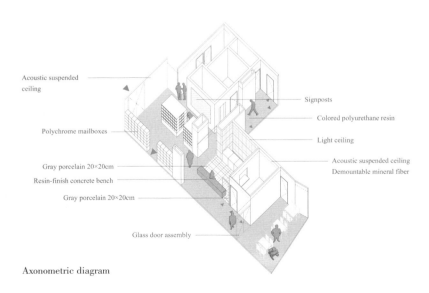

Acoustic suspended ceiling

Polychrome mailboxes

Gray porcelain 20×20cm

Resin-finish concrete bench

Gray porcelain 20×20cm

Glass door assembly

Signposts

Colored polyurethane resin

Light ceiling

Acoustic suspended ceiling
Demountable mineral fiber

Axonometric diagram

"We try to approach every project individually based upon the parameters of the site, client, budget, and program."

Daryl Olesinski, Martina Linden

Daryl Olesinski attended the University of Wisconsin-Milwaukee, receiving a Bachelor of Science in Architecture. After completing his undergraduate studies, Olesinski received his Masters of Art in Architecture from the Southern California Institute of Architecture. The first few years of his professional life were spent working for various Architectural firms throughout the City of Los Angeles. Throughout his seventeen-year career, Olesinski has had the opportunity to construct several buildings, which has been critical to his education within the profession. He started his own practice in 2003, partnering with his wife, Martina Linden and they have been in practice together for over ten years.

The design aesthetic of their studio, O+ L Building Projects LLC is a subtle, clean, and elegant regional modernism. Their work centers on the building's ability to spatially expand beyond its walls into gardens and patios to capture natural light and views of the natural landscape. Committed to the advancement of regional modern design inherent to Southern California, Olesinski and Linden both believe that the integration of the built space with the outdoors is at the heart of Southern California residential design.

PROJECT NAME---Ravoli Residence
LOCATION---Pacific Palisades, California, United States
COMPLETED---2018
AREA---13,650 square feet (1,268 square meters)
DESIGN---O+ L Building Projects LLC
PHOTOGRAPHY---Todd Goodman (LA Light Photography)

Ravoli Residence sits on a sloping block in the heart of Pacific Palisades and was conceived as a California Modernist estate. Narrow at street level and widening toward the rear, the two-story building appears as a single-story structure from the street. It widens to create a wing typology with each wing reaching into the site to capture garden spaces, frame views, and accommodate service amenities.

A series of site walls and fencing define the property edge and create privacy from the street. The entry to the house is through a descending garden that enjoys a view through the house to the slopes of the Will

Rogers State Historic Park beyond. Shaped as a modified T, the six-bedroom house extends into the landscape, creating separate wings dedicated to the programming of the building. The residence includes formal entryways, living and dining area, as well as a large entertainment-style kitchen, family room, library, theater, wine cellar, and a selection of fitness and wellness spaces plus guesthouse. Interior spaces are balanced with large exterior decks, patios, and a pool.

A stately 80-foot-tall (24-meter-tall) eucalyptus tree inspired the colors, tones, and textures of the material palette. Expansive use of glass balances the solidity of the board-formed concrete walls and the warm tones of stained wood siding throughout the building. The remainder of the building is wrapped in colored, steel-troweled stucco. Doors disappear into internal pockets and the flooring extends onto decks and patios to create a seamless relationship between the interior and exterior—house to land.

North elevation

How do you resolve the unfavorable aspects of site conditions?

The way our office approaches all projects is to start with an extensive site analysis. The time spent in the study informs our design process in ways that we really do not even fully understand until the design is worked through. In this study, we learn the inherently good and bad qualities of a property, whether it be great views, traffic noise, a nice natural breeze, or the way the sun moves across the site to provide natural light. This study shows us how the design can either mask the bad or reinforce the good.

How do you put forward solutions comprehensively and objectively without any prejudgments?

We try very hard to not bring any preconceived ideas to the table or repeat ourselves and other work we have done. We dislike when, after being on-site for ten minutes, we are asked what the building will look like; or when someone says they want another of the buildings we have already done.

Sections

Each project, like each person, is individual and should be approached as such. Time to study and consider are critical to the design process.

How do you perceive the abstract architectural space?

I feel it is inherent to all architects and designers to be able to see three-dimensionally and understand the importance of proportion and scale in both plan and section. The challenge is not to have the architect or designer be able to understand these relationships, but the clients. With the technology readily available today, the ability to provide your clients both modeling and imagery in the form of 3D visualizations and physical modeling is a critical tool to have. When working on projects in the office, we try to use as many of these tools as possible through both physical and digital modeling. We find that most clients do not really fully understand the space, proportions, and scale of the buildings and their individual spaces until

they actually walk through the project while it is being built. To mitigate this as best as possible, our office uses the power of 3D modeling software and rendering visualizations to digitally place the clients in the buildings and individual spaces of the buildings. For Ravoli Residence, we utilized physical modeling and 3D digital modeling to convey the building in design and during construction phases.

How do you coordinate the relationship between function, space, style, and circulation?

The organization of the spaces and functions plays a critical role in our design process. We see this as a natural extension of how the building relates to the site, its context, micro– and macroclimate, and how the user of the building, therefore, relates to the building and, by extension, the place they live in. I am not sure that the proper word to use is "coordinate" as much it would be "compose." As a design office, our architectural works are based upon an understanding of the site and the building's relationship to that site. The relationship

of function, quality of space, and how one moves through the building and site are all intertwined, hence the building and site planning. As for the Ravoli Residence, we utilized a series of interlocking and adjacent spaces that move down the site's natural slope and which directly open out onto the garden and patio terraces. We limited the idea of "circulation" as much as possible and let the spaces flow from one to the other. As outlined above, the composition of a space and flow of programming is critical to the way we plan our buildings.

How do your plans and ideas contribute in deriving a design?

While our office does keep a record of everything we do, we try to approach every project individually, based upon the parameters of the site, client, budget, and program. While we will look back to previous projects for inspiration and/or ideas, this is a small part of how we approach design.

How do you try to understand your clients' intentions?

When our office is approached to take on a project, typically the clients already have a piece of land upon which to build. A large part of what we do as designers is to understand why the owners were drawn to that property and what the design can do to reinforce those aspects of the site. We do not believe that the clients have "intentions," rather, we firmly believe that there is a strong draw to a piece of property that acts as the reason that the owners purchased it to begin with.

How do you incorporate your client's proposals into your design schemes?

We typically do not enter into a project with preconceived ideas. However, the clients may, and a part of the work takes those ideas into account. We make judgments as to the validity of the ideas, as some of them may not actually work and some of them may not be good to start with. Marrying their ideas with the ideas that we create in response to

the design problem is a part of the overall design process. Sometimes, the ideas the owners have make their way into the final product, and sometimes they do not.

Every residential project comes with the owners' ideas and thoughts on how they would design the house. As the design office, we balance the ideas the owners have with the way the site itself wants to be developed. We do not approach the design of our buildings with a heavy hand to a big pen. The owners know how they live and the lifestyle they have more than we do and as such, their ideas need to be given weight.

With respect to Ravoli Residence, we were given a great deal of freedom to create and were almost never questioned or told "no." However, there were design elements that we had in our minds that the owner did not agree with. The family room and kitchen receive a great deal of direct sunlight. As such, we knew that these spaces could get quite warm in the summer months. So, as a part of the design and engineering process, we designed a steel trellis to cover the family room terrace and reduce the amount of direct sunlight on these spaces. The owner did not agree with limiting the view toward the sky out of these doors and as such, decided not to build that portion of the project. We felt very strongly that this was a necessary element for the house but the reality is, the designer or architect are not the owner, and while we can make the argument about these decisions, ultimately, they are not ours to make.

How do you make evaluations and judgments on your own schemes?

We are always looking at the design in a critical manner throughout the design process. No idea is perfect, nor cannot be improved with a bit of editing and clarification. It is important to be able to self-evaluate your ideas without losing the intent of the idea, and to be able to change direction if the way in which those ideas are being manifested is critical to the success of the building. There are literally thousands of decisions that are made on every building and to be able to look at those decisions critically is an integral part of the way we work.

We perform the schematic design process and do an internal review, and discuss the project as designed before we meet with the clients. As architects and designers, we learn from every project we take on. Some lessons are good, some are bad. To be able to self-evaluate your own work is critical to growing as a designer. The challenge with the Ravoli Residence was about how far to take the design. The building was designed for the speculative market, so it had to walk

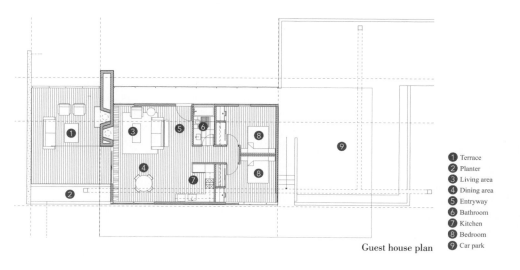

Guest house plan

1 Terrace
2 Planter
3 Living area
4 Dining area
5 Entryway
6 Bathroom
7 Kitchen
8 Bedroom
9 Car park

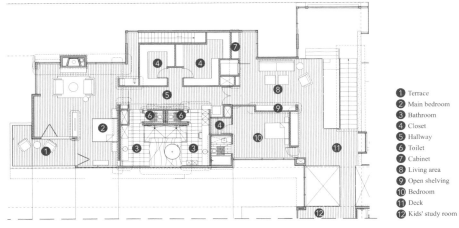

Second-floor plan

1 Terrace
2 Main bedroom
3 Bathroom
4 Closet
5 Hallway
6 Toilet
7 Cabinet
8 Living area
9 Open shelving
10 Bedroom
11 Deck
12 Kids' study room

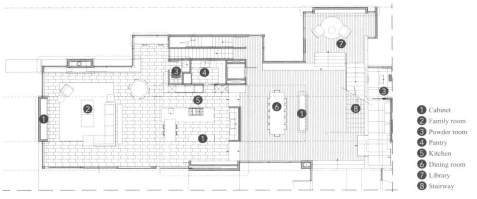

First-floor plan

1 Cabinet
2 Family room
3 Powder room
4 Pantry
5 Kitchen
6 Dining room
7 Library
8 Stairway

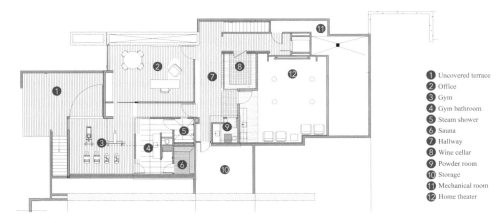

Basement plan

1 Uncovered terrace
2 Office
3 Gym
4 Gym bathroom
5 Steam shower
6 Sauna
7 Hallway
8 Wine cellar
9 Powder room
10 Storage
11 Mechanical room
12 Home theater

a fine line between being an interesting piece of modern residential architecture, and still safe and "usual" enough to appeal to the widest range of buyers. In this context, we had to make several decisions for materials that caused us to meticulously examine our design work.

How do you stay curious in complex and disordered situations?

To remain curious about all aspects of design and architecture is fundamental to the pursuit of this profession. The process is, by its nature, complex, with many different parts to think about, and all at the same time; making order out of the disorder is inherent in that. Sifting through the non-critical information and arriving at the heart of the design problem is the basis of our work.

To be able to see through the chaos and disorder and focus on both the big picture and the finest of details is critical to this process. Complexity and disorder are a part of this process and to have the stamina to deal with it is critical to a successful project. Workload and fatigue are real issues and relying on easy go-to solutions that you have done before is not unusual. However, to stay original and true to the vision of the design, you need to stay motivated. With Ravoli Residence, we worked with a good team of builders who always pushed us to go further with the design. We tried

as much as possible not to repeat ourselves. Yes, there is a similarity to other work that we have created and there are some building systems that are used over and over, but this is a result of the experience of working with local tradesmen and understanding them and their skill set.

When designing, not all of an architect's ideas can always be fully realized. Could you share on how to handle such a situation?

You are right, in every building there are several ideas that are not realized for various reasons. These ideas always stay in the back of your mind for later use on another project. There are so many reasons why a particular idea cannot be realized on a particular project that you have little or no control over. This does not make them bad ideas, rather, these become the foundation for another building that can see the benefit of that original idea in a new way. There will always be another opportunity to utilize these ideas in some form sometime in the future. Never give up, never stop trying, and never settle for mediocrity.

When you worked on this project, how did you strive to maintain your original idea from beginning to end?

The design process never stops, even up to the point that the building is being built. If the inherent ideas mentioned are strong, there should be no need to stop. Basing the design ideas on real-world physical characteristics drives the reasoning behind the building. There is literally a reason for everything that is done, and when those decisions are founded in sound reason and extensive analysis, making a change in direction should not involve the basis of the design ideas.

How do you make a comprehensive judgment on a design's progress and optimize the process?

Making judgments about the work you do is how a design, in general, works. You have an idea, and you work that idea until you can make the judgment on its success. There is a great deal of stepping forward and then stepping back based upon the reaction the idea created. Don't be afraid to leave an idea and start over, or use some of that idea toward a different solution. Design is messy and to be able to edit critically is very important.

How do you identify critical problems and seek solutions?

The recognition that there are always issues that the design is trying to solve is integral to every design process. They are called design problems for a reason and the ability for the building to solve them is what is at the heart of good architecture. O+ L sees the design process as a journey to the right solution for that individual site, program, budget, and client. Each of those factors is at the core of how we work for every project we take on. Sometimes, all these work together, and sometimes, they work in conflict, but no matter what, the building created needs to solve these to be successful.

What role does teamwork play in identifying problems that may have been overlooked?

At O+ L, we do not see the design process as having an end, even after the building is built. There are always lessons to learn and knowledge to be gained throughout the process. From working as a team in the office and bouncing ideas off each other, to using the expertise of the labor and tradesmen to better understand how the details can be built, there are always additional conditions to recognize, analyze, and solve that require more knowledge and or experience than you have. Designing and constructing a building is by no means a singular act that can be done by one person. It takes many people, each with their own understanding of what their role is to make the ideas created on paper a reality. Searching out those problems throughout the process is critical to a building's success.

How do you respond to unexpected problems that occur during the design process?

Every project, no matter how big or small, expensive or budget-driven, has issues to overcome. This is expected;

with so many different criteria and so many rules and regulations, there will always be issues to overcome. It is best to assume this from the start and not be disappointed when it happens.

At the start of every project, we consider all the issues that might arise and try to do as much research as possible into the potential issues and incorporate them into the work. With that said, there will be problems that you, as an architect or designer, will need to be able to work around. Sometimes, those very problems actually demand the most creative solutions. Whether it be reconsidering the structure, how the building engages the site, or how best to deal with materials to satisfy a budget, you will need to be able to understand and adapt to meet those challenges. Even when you think you have solved all the problems and the building is in construction, there will be outside influences, such as client changes or governing agency issues, that you will need to be able to incorporate into the final building. The only time something is done is when it is actually done.

"We think through sketches."

murmuro

João Caldas and Rita Breda cofounded murmuro, working from Braga and Porto in Portugal. Caldas and Breda began their design journey together at the University of Coimbra, studying in the Department of Architecture (DARQ-FCT). As Erasmus students at the Trondheim Academy of Fine Art at the Norwegian University of Science and Technology, they had the opportunity to take part in an interdisciplinary and collaborative program for architecture and art students, which was pivotal in their education. The success of their projects led to the founding of murmuro in 2015, where they develop projects regardless of their scale, program, or budget.

PROJECT NAME---Colégio dos Plátanos
LOCATION---Sintra, Portugal
COMPLETED---2017
AREA---19,913 square feet (1,850 square meters)
DESIGN---murmuro
PHOTOGRAPHY---Pedro Nuno Pacheco

Colégio dos Plátanos consisted of the expansion and reorganization of the school, which educates children aged three to fourteen years old. Having acquired a set of low-quality buildings east of the existing school, the client intended to demolish them and expand the school, adding new classrooms, complementary spaces, and sports facilities. However, the client changed course during the design phase, deciding to keep the buildings and instead, construct a smaller building to connect the west and east parts of the school. The construction had to occur in two phases and, therefore, required the development of an intermediate structural solution and controlled demolitions in order not to disrupt

daily school operation. Only with the conclusion of the second phase was the entire complex complete.

The new building is simultaneously a connection and an articulation point. It connects the east and west buildings and articulates the levels of the outdoor courtyard to the south, sports area to the north, and covered outdoor area to the east.

Natural ventilation was a requisite for the design, as well as the protection of the northern openings, given the proximity to the sports area. Murmuro created a permeable brick façade that allows natural ventilation in the building, illuminates the northern rooms, protects the windows, and hides the necessary ventilation grids. Exterior shading slabs and interior screens to the south control the intensity of the light in the classrooms.

Inside, preschool classrooms are covered in cheerful, brightly colored panels. Walls are coated with a material that allows acoustic conditioning and can be used for the display of children's works.

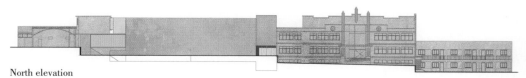

North elevation

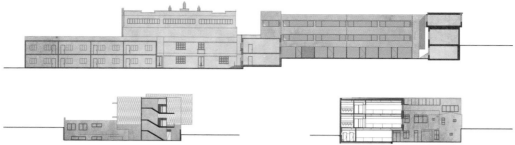

Sections

How do you resolve the unfavorable aspects of site conditions?

At murmuro, we do not approach site conditions as unfavourable factors or negative hurdles to be overcome. Those circumstances, as well as social and economic specificities of a given project, are a starting point and, in fact, they are what give meaning to architecture, both in terms of aesthetics and functionality.

How do you put forward solutions comprehensively and objectively without any prejudgments?

Each project has its own identity. Our design process is always accompanied by a research procedure. We do not work on preconceived ideas or specific concepts that guide or limit the project. We take into consideration all the factors, and together with our creativity and culture, we come up with an answer in the form of a building space.

For example, we try to unveil the design solutions from a close analysis of the site, the existing architectural heritage, the socioeconomic scenario, or the specific demands of the client. We work with a multidisciplinary approach focused on the client's requirements, applicable laws, the genius loci, as well as the aesthetic consistency, durability, and future lifespan of the buildings. The development of the design of Colégio dos Plátanos followed that script.

1. Zinc sheet flashing
2. Ceiling ventilation duct
3. Metallic ventilation grid
4. Metallic structure for brick
5. Permeable brick façade
6. Metallic slab
7. Exterior window frames
8. Courtyard drainage grill

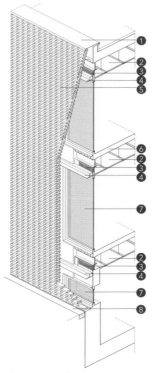

Axonometric diagram

How do you perceive the abstract architectural space?

The exercise of relating your body with the spaces you conceptualize in your mind must be driven by a physical notion of proportion and measurement equilibrium. The continuous exercise of tape measuring our surroundings in our office and in our building sites and the unconscious physical relation to objects through your hand span dimension are both personal devices to get a mental notion of the space. This enables you to move within the conceptions of space you create.

How do you coordinate the relationship between function, space, style, and circulation?

One of the most crucial requirement of the expansion of Colégio dos Plátanos was that the new building had to function as an articulation point between the east- and west-existing buildings at different levels. Therefore, our project works as a bridge that links pre-existent

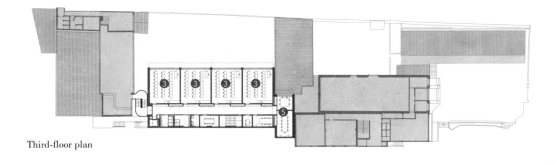

Third-floor plan

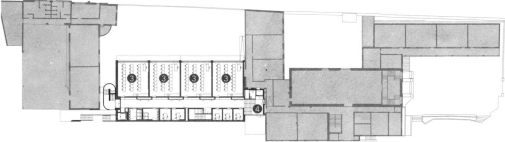

Second-floor plan

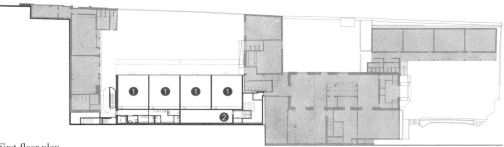

First-floor plan

1 Preschool
2 Storage room
3 Classrooms
4 Entrance
5 Meeting room

conditions, not only in terms of function, but also in terms of circulation. This is particularly clear on the design of the west staircase: at an intermediate level, it defines the entrance path from the playground and the link to the west-existing building, and at the first-floor level, it assures the circulation continuity to the new classrooms and the link to the east-existing building.

How do your plans and ideas contribute in deriving a design?

Try to stay curious through the process, always reassuring the basic principles that guide your main idea with new schemes, diagrams, and illustrations. The design process will have unexpected shifts that will test and reinforce your decisions. In Colégio dos Plátanos, the initial briefing of the client was not stable through the whole process. The client made crucial decisions throughout the process that impelled drastic shifts in the design. For example, the client decided to maintain the east-existing building, which was initially intended to be demolished. This fact forced us to rethink the circulation scheme and develop a new staircase enclosed in a concrete volume that could articulate the accesses to the two buildings (the new and the old) and ensure the volumetric equilibrium in the transition between such different architectonic realities.

How do you try to understand your clients' intentions?

The dialogue between the parties at play in the design process is essential to a deeper understanding of the commission. For example, during the design phase of Colégio dos Plátanos, the client changed the parameters of the project by deciding to maintain some existing buildings, thereby reducing the investment and demanding a division of construction into two phases. This fact had an enormous impact on the course of the design, leading us to a new structural scheme (a steel frame structure), a divided plan for demolitions, and even the developing of ephemeral access devices (to be demolished in the second phase).

How do you incorporate your client's proposals into your design schemes?

The conceptual intentions of a project are multiple levels. Architecture is not driven by an exclusively aesthetic gesture. Above all, it is a process of reordering a multiplicity of problems, inconsistencies, and contradictions—a

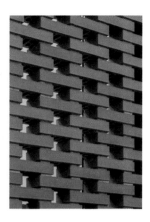

complexity that is often only translated in abstract schemes or sketches that incorporate meanings and relationships without any physical image in mind. The client's proposals or requirements are in fact one of the starting points of our research. They exist in our design schemes as fundamental circumstances and are the cornerstones that drive the design solutions. They may be at times challenging, and it's up to our professional experience to give them an answer, or perhaps, explain and present a counter solution that is in the best interest of the project and client—which happens at times and is always well received.

In Colégio dos Plátanos, the hit-and-miss brick façade, one of the most characteristic features of the building, emerged from the client's requirement to avoid mechanical ventilation systems so as to maintain every square meter of the sports area. Hence, we came up with this solution, which both protects the needed windows from the sports activities and allows us to implement a natural ventilation system in the northern façade, taking advantage of the dominant winds. We also had to maintain all the existent buildings; our buildings, therefore, had to connect all these different levels, which was added difficulty. We also had to plan the construction in two different phases (imposed by the specific economic context of Portugal in 2008/2009), and that made us rethink the constructive system and paths as the second phase was built while the first phase was being used. All of the client's requirements led us to be more resourceful, and to aim higher on our solutions.

How do you make evaluations and judgments on your own schemes?

The conclusions you come up with must always be tested. There are unpredictable variables along the way that have to be taken into account and one should not develop the design process as a closed container. Even after the conclusion of the construction projects, small tweaks are made in order to adjust to new conditions on the site. From the most simple and abstract scheme to the detailed construction drawing, re-evaluation is key.

There is a continuous strategy of testing our design solutions through different types of sketches—from perspective sketches that emulate the living experience of the space and its proportions, to constructive detailed drawings searching for the best constructive solution. Fundamentally, one must always have a way of continuously testing the solutions that they arrive at. At the end of the day, everything is traceable back to a consistent set of concerns, such as mass, volume, proportion, geometry, repetition, light, and those that transform the physical space into something to be experienced.

How do you stay curious in complex and disordered situations?

Do not fall into despair in complex situations. Absorb new conditions as an opportunity to think differently and develop inventive solutions. But never lose order and coordination. Architects usually act as project coordinators, combining the different input and labors of different technicians. From engineers to the contractors, they all rely on your coordination power to make things go forward. Complexity is never a synonym with disorder.

When designing, not all of an architect's ideas can always be fully realized. Could you share on how to handle such a situation?

Through the continuous search for cutting-edge construction methods and the enrichment of our office's library under a pedagogical stance of our practice. Our design process has before denied a catalog of preconceived ideas and concepts. We harbor no nostalgic feelings toward unrealizable ideas as they are not the suitable solution for the problem we are trying to solve. Therefore, if it doesn't provide the best answer to our problem/project, it is not the correct path that we must take.

The design process is an act of thinking, testing, and analyzing throughout a period of time where concepts and ideas are continuously being validated and, sometimes, thrown away. The way we deal with unrealized ideas is as simple as that.

When you worked on this project, how did you strive to maintain your original idea from beginning to end?

We think through sketches. However, this drawing habit can sometimes be driven by the enjoyment of an unconscious illustrative treat that results in deviating from its main goal. If so, you must find new ways of analyzing your project. Physical models are an excellent way of getting a notion of scale in your design. But, you should also develop your own ways of stopping when you start getting complicated solutions to complex problems. Don't be afraid to reboot the process because after, you always restart with a wider knowledge of the problem.

We believe that in architecture, ideas and concepts must not be stable or immutable. They are continuously evolving throughout a process of sedimentation and perfecting. Your initial idea is an abstract approximation to the final realization of the building. In fact, a good idea is one that is able to absorb new information you gather through research for the project and change without compromising the overall definition of the project. We don't focus on the importance of an original idea as we believe architecture is not about the starting point. It is about the journey of each project and all its layers.

How do you make a comprehensive judgment on a design's progress and optimize the process?

The constant evaluation of your design decisions impels a natural definition of the steady gestures and the ones that need to be tuned. You should be open to reconsider, avoiding dogmatic decisions. Exercise profound analysis of the reality you are working with and avoid the misconceptions that a construction based on abstract ideas and concepts can create. In Colégio dos Plátanos, the exercise of "reading" the site was complex and long. As we were working with pre-existing buildings and exterior spaces with different functions and elevations, all the design was developed within this process of discovering the site. The ideas for the new building became clearer the sharper our knowledge of the site became. It was a process of comparing, contrasting, and judging our design decisions with a "scenario" that already existed and had to be optimized.

How do you identify critical problems and seek solutions?
The self-evaluation gets narrower as the problem analysis extends deeper. Our practice is based on a critical perspective toward the commission you get. Sometimes your client is not fully aware of the complexity of their

requirements. You should seek for problems beyond the ones that are initially presented to you. In Colégio dos Plátanos, the use of a hit-and-miss brick façade solved problems of durability and resistance as the north façade was facing a sports courtyard heavily used by the school students. It was not included in the initial briefing of the client.

What role does teamwork play in identifying problems that may have been overlooked?

The act of designing and building is a collective one. From the architects in our team who are involved, to the several engineering teams and contractors, it is always an act of collective coordination and cooperation between different professionals, each one with their special ability to identify and solve different problems throughout the designing and construction process. We, as architects, are the conductors of the orchestra.

How do you respond to unexpected problems that occur during the design process?

As we explained earlier, architectural designing for us is an act of continuous research, which allows us to get through all the unexpected circumstances that we did not predict when we sketched the initial idea. The question is not how you respond to unexpected problems, but how you define a design process that is able to manage unexpected circumstances as crucial points of input to the design, because one does not fully know all the layers of problems that may need to be solved when we sketch an initial concept. Usually, when an unexpected problem arises, first we take a break, then we think. No doubt, sometimes, there are a few seconds of panic or disappointment in between, depending on the seriousness of the unexpected problem, but that is just human nature. It is not a matter of anticipating problems, but enjoying the process of solving them. And that is the fun part of it!

"Develop the project in parallel paths, proposing different alternatives on each aspect of the project."

Marcelo Ruiz Pardo

Marcelo Ruiz Pardo, cofounder of Ruiz Pardo, studied architecture at the Superior Technical School of Architecture of Madrid (ETSAM) and the University of Geneva. Ruiz Pardo is a lecturer of architectural design at ETSAM, where he is also a PhD candidate and a member of several research groups, innovation teaching groups, and development cooperation groups. He has been a visiting critic and lecturer at international universities in the United States, Japan, Hong Kong, El Salvador, and Puerto Rico. Ruiz Pardo has also been a part of seminars and conferences at international congresses about university teaching.

PROJECT NAME---Fronton Bizkaia, Basque handball courts
LOCATION---Bilbao, Spain
COMPLETED---2011
AREA---258,452 square feet (24,011 square meters)
DESIGN---Marcelo Ruiz Pardo (Ruiz Pardo – Nebreda), Javier Gastón
PHOTOGRAPHY---Jesús Granada
AWARDS---Architecture MasterPrize 2016, Honorable Mention

Fronton Bizkaia is located on the outskirts of the city. One side fronts the terraced land, countryside, mountains, and road to the city. The other side faces adjacent residential blocks and the park to the south. The design plays with volume and scale to link with its immediate surroundings and distant scenery. Thus, the nearly blind façade facing the highway becomes a perforated form in its contact with the houses, or with the large vertical voids that allow light to enter the office area.

The materials blend with various shapes in the surrounding environment, and the traditional stacking of a stone base and a

lightweight construction frame is reversed to achieve a closer and warmer contact. Cedar cladding around the base creates a more human scale for passersby, and the mass of black slate appears as an abstract object when viewed from afar.

The interior of the building is divided into two parts according to use: the office area and the sports area, which includes the fronton court, *trinquete*, and spectator stands. The interior is a continuous open space that transitions from the compression of the corridors to the expanded areas designed for sports and congregation. It is a fluid and porous space with divisions that are hardly perceptible, and yet manage to segment different uses of space.

The space is strictly defined by the structure—a series of concrete walls and shielding pillars that support the stepped seating platforms that are superimposed upon each other. The metallic roof structure comprising wide-edged steel trusses rests on the enclosing perimeter walls. Deep skylights are carved out of the roof and ceiling structure, and lighting is concentrated in the narrow bands in between, creating rhythm and pattern.

At the southern end of the building, there is an independent access to the office area, which is connected to the rest of the interior via a service bay. Deep vertical shafts bring in natural light while protecting the interior from direct sunlight. The trident layout of the office floors means each bay receives light from two angles. A large functional surface area is gained from a compact form, avoiding the appearance of very recessed areas of work, while preserving the overall shape of the building.

The perforations in the building's solid mass emit light at night, as light seeps out via holes from of its hollow interior, giving a sense of the activity within.

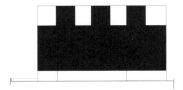 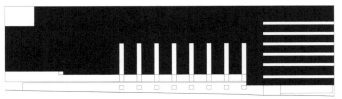

Elevations

How do you resolve the unfavorable aspects of site conditions?

Site constraints are opportunities to make something unique and special. Therefore, unfavorable factors are not something to be resolved, but situations that may enrich your project. Instead of trying to impose pre-fixed ideas to a specific context, it is more productive to think of how to make the project possible given the particular challenge. In any case, the place is not just the physical support of an environment. The place is also built by the underlying relationships—that is, their cultural ties, the craft tradition, or their social background, among others. The location of Fronton Bizkaia was one with great potential. The building is located on the outskirts of the city at the far end of the urban extension of Bilbao's Miribilla district. One side faces the terraced land, the countryside, the mountains, and the access road to the city. The other side faces adjacent residential blocks and the park in the south. The design plays with volume and scale such that it links with its immediate surroundings and the distant scenery.

How do you put forward solutions comprehensively and objectively without any prejudgments?

A good project is not made only by the correct integration of functional requirements. It is much more than a problem-solving issue. Every project brief receives a different, unique spin on design. It could be something based on your own research or points of interest in order to make the design appealing and personalized, so as to connect with the user's needs, and to build a new reality around it. In the Fronton Bizkaia project, it was very important to take into account the tradition of the game and the space in which it takes place, and its roots in the collective identity. Project decisions—from the materials, to the character of the congregation space itself—did not obey purely functional issues, but rather, the desire to create an atmosphere that identifies with traditional spaces while having a contemporary reading.

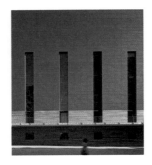

How do you perceive the abstract architectural space?

The project Fronton Bizkaia, which has a 3,000-person capacity, was designed considering their movement across the building. The interior space is a continuous and open space ranging sequentially from the compression of the corridors to the expanded areas designed for congregation and sport. An interior landscape has been created replete with visual and spatial connections. The internal space is fluid and porous with divisions that are hardly perceptible, yet nevertheless manage to segment different uses of space. Moreover, architecture is not only about form and function. These days, it is more about the potential of the space. You will have to think about how the projects evolve in time. It will have to deal with uncertainty and, therefore, it will have to allow change and movement.

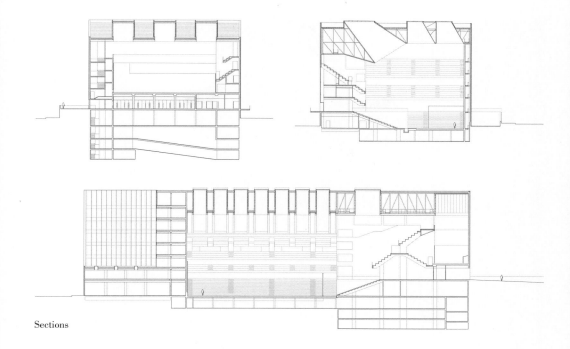

Sections

How do you coordinate the relationship between function, space, style, and circulation?

Develop the project in parallel paths, proposing different alternatives on each aspect of the project. In this way, the process is enriched with new variables. Little by little this development in parallel will find points of confluence to develop one or more proposals. These are projects built with layers. Fronton Bizkaia has the complexity of a professional arena, and this involves managing many different circulation paths (spectators, players, media, and so on), as well as functional needs. To operate through layers was very useful.

How do your plans and ideas contribute in deriving a design?

To develop a project is a research activity. Therefore, you will never know how the project will be until you complete it. It is made in the making and consequently, the process becomes capital. There is no such thing as the "idea" to be reached, but the process to be explored. This does not end

with the project, but continues on with the construction on-site. It is an open process, not only in relation to the final result, but also in relation to the agents that participate in it. The exercise of professional activity as an architect does not take place in solitude; there are a large number of "actors" who participate. From consultants and collaborators, to specialists, investors, technicians, and users, among others. The project forms a network between all of them and the architect must be able to coordinate all their input.

How do you try to understand your clients' intentions?

The client has to feel satisfied and identify with the project. This is not incompatible with making good architecture. The challenge here is to put the client's wills and desires into great architectural proposals without limiting their participation in the project. Fronton Bizkaia is a public building and in these particular cases, the client is the society as whole, which is much more complex. The expectations were very high as this is a very popular game in this region. For this reason, it was very important to understand the cultural roots of the game.

How do you incorporate your client's proposals into your design schemes?

It is important to understand the figure of the architect as an instrument of dialogue capable of establishing links between different agents. Regardless of the context, the figure of the architect must be the catalyst that brings together the visions and interests of all agents, and to translate them into architectural propositions.

How do you make evaluations and judgments on your own schemes?

All project processes are a back-and-forth path. It is important to keep a critical attitude toward your own work without losing perspective.

It is important to open your eyes and see your work as if looking at it for the very first time. Like fish, which do not see the water, we routinely act without questioning the parameters that determine the framework within which we proceed in our projects. Seeing and describing your own work as though you have never seen it before, is a radical and transforming act that requires an exercise of estrangement aimed at judging and questioning that which is taken as established. The recognition of this reality is essential to working in a conscious, constructive, and alternative manner.

How do you stay curious in complex and disordered situations?

Fronton Bizkaia had to have a complex structural solution although it appears very simple. This result was achieved

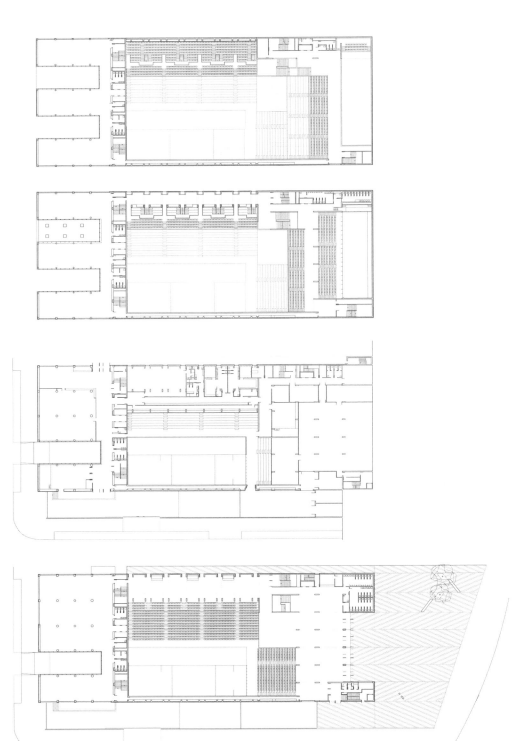

Floor plans

through mixed structures and integrating MEP facilities within a large span, and the will of keeping them unnoticed. The most valuable creative solutions always arise in complex situations where typical solutions prove unsuitable. These situations are opportunities to think differently and to propose the unexpected.

When designing, not all of an architect's ideas can always be fully realized. Could you share on how to handle such a situation?

You should always distinguish between simple and simplistic design solutions. An effective, simple solution should be direct and straightforward, uncomplicated, and feasible. As Anne Lacaton and Jean-Philippe Vassal have stated, "Architecture will be straightforward, useful, precise, cheap, free, jovial, poetic, and cosmopolitan."

When you worked on this project, how did you strive to maintain your original idea from beginning to end?

As mentioned before, creative design is more like a research activity to discover paths that have not been explored

before. Consequently, it can be difficult to define what the direction of the design is. Nevertheless, you should have some milestones or conceptual reference points in order to navigate and negotiate the uncertainty of a design process with a coherent criterion. For the Fronton project, some key elements were fixed as concepts—for example, obtaining natural light through skylights—but the design solutions evolved and varied several times.

How do you make a comprehensive judgment on a design's progress and optimize the process?

Sometimes, the optimization of the design can lead to the project not evolving or incorporating improvements in the process. For the Fronton project, we made visuals of the playing area and countless sections of the stands with different access points for the spectators. Many of them were similar, but each brought something different. When working with a large number of solutions, an evolutionary process occurs. In this case, many sections were discarded, but many others were integrated until the final section was consolidated. The design process should be a balance between optimized and unoptimized situations. Creative design processes are unoptimized by definition. Otherwise, creativity can easily be learned by artificial intelligence.

How do you identify critical problems and seek solutions?

A project should be on permanent revision from its conceptual stage until its completion. With a flexible and adaptable attitude, solutions will arise immediately if needed. The design should be good enough to withstand minor alterations and keep its nature at the same time.

What role does teamwork play in identifying problems that may have been overlooked?

Teamwork requires commitment and dialogue. In a context where each professional only attends to his or her area

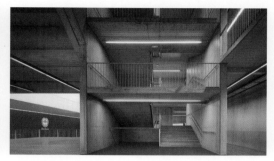

of responsibility, projects will become unmanageable. The more effective way to engage everyone involved in a project is to make them believe that they are taking part in something special and that their participation is critical for its success. When we worked on Fronton Bizkaia, we had meetings with professional players, referees, sports commentators, and even technicians. Each of them brought to light to something we didn't notice before. This process was very important to enrich and complete the project.

How do you respond to unexpected problems that occur during the design process?

Unexpected problems are completely expected. It is important to learn to face projects and work with great flexibility and adaptability. A project is a script that must be completed and enriched throughout its execution.

"An architect should be capable of constantly questioning their own work, as well as allowing it to be questioned by others during the entire design process."

AAP

Rui Miguel Vargas, Abdulatif Almishari

Rui Miguel Vargas studied in Instituto Superior Manuel Teixeira Gomes (ISMAT) and graduated from Milan Polytechnic Institute in 2000. In 2003, he cofounded ORV, based in Faro, Portugal. He is a practicing and principal architect at the Associated Architects Partnership (AAP), based in Kuwait and Portugal, which operates in several countries.

Abdulatif Almishari is a practicing architect and principal at AAP. He is a member of the Kuwait 2035 Vision Committee of the Supreme Council of Planning and Development of the State of Kuwait. Almishari earned his Bachelor of Architecture from the University of Southern California and his Master's of Architecture from Harvard University's Graduate School of Design.

PROJECT NAME---Areia
LOCATION---Al Khiran, Kuwait
COMPLETED---2017
AREA---22,206 square feet
(2,063 square meters)
DESIGN---Associated Architects Partnership (AAP)
PHOTOGRAPHY---João Morgado
AWARDS---The Architecture MasterPrize 2018 in Residential Architecture; The Chicago Athenaeum International Architecture Awards 2019 in Multi-family Housing

In the late 1990s, infrastructural development along the Kuwaiti coastline began to take shape as a new master plan for the new city of Al Khiran was registered. A network of artificial canals and lagoons was constructed to increase the number of waterfront plots, each with a small slice of the beach and street access to the distribution road. Small family dwellings became desirable for weekends and holidays, and to fulfill the needs of the traditional Kuwaiti family seeking non-permanent housing.

Areia is a residential development consisting of five residences on five plots of land. The program of each residence interprets the Kuwaiti way

of life, relating the main day-to-day living areas to the beach, patios, gardens, and pool areas. The *diwaniya*, a formal social gathering space for guests, is next to the entrance. The upper floors are more enclosed to provide privacy for the bedrooms, but still offer views of the city.

The five villas have the same organizational concept. However, their volumetric compositions present gentle variations that make each house unique. When seen from the road, they appear as a simple repetition of the same house, while a more heterogeneous façade is experienced from the canal.

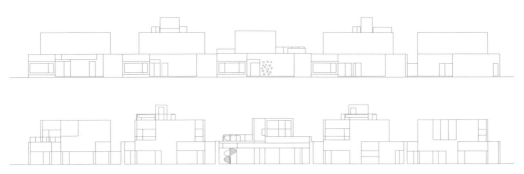

Sections

How do you resolve the unfavorable aspects of site conditions?

Areia is located in Sabah Alahmed Alsabah Maritime City in the southern part of Kuwait. The habitability conditions and service infrastructures, having been developed from scratch, created an artificial scenario destined for unpredictable diversity. The area brings the sea into the desert by creating a series of canals that are anchored by docks and marinas, and which is livened by other recreational activities. The need to design architecture within an undefined context was both a challenge and an opportunity to explore the facets of place creation through architectural space.

How do you put forward solutions comprehensively and objectively without any prejudgments?

From an early stage, the idea was to develop a sense of unity, using the same architectural language of simple plane geometry, as well as the same basic concept and programmatic organization. This resulted in a contemporary image of continuity and proportion, where slight harmonious variations guarantee complexity and diversity to the houses.

This simple and neutral approach tried to restore use, function, and habitability to the basic shaded courtyard typology in comparison with the architectural anarchy of the developing city, where different residential designs with variations in color, dimensions, form, texture, and structural solution create a complex, heterogeneous collage of a place that is still undefined.

How do you perceive the abstract architectural space?

The sense of experiencing a space, or a sequence of spaces, is something that is part of the creative process. Areia is developed with a certain ability to foresee the users' movements and the sensations that can be stimulated by these spaces. However, in order to reach its full potential, the need for human interaction and involvement with the space is required.

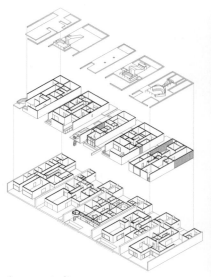

Axonometric diagram

How do you coordinate the relationship between function, space, style, and circulation?

Architecture is the whole and cannot be seen as a sum of its different parts. The initial program dictates the limits and requirements that proposed solutions need to fulfill in order to solve the design problem. This initial programmatic analysis is the starting point in the process of creation. From there, the various project necessities, preoccupations, legal requirements, client tastes, and a myriad of other elements are combined, contrasted, set apart, and hidden, in service of the greater idea. In this particular project, we decided to manipulate the program in different ways, repositioning certain elements in order to create five solutions regarding the principal idea. This resulted in variable programmatic articulations and habitability conditions. Each house becomes unique and at the same time, part of the set that includes all five houses. The role of the architect is like that of a conductor—maintaining this complex orchestra in time and in tune to the original idea.

How do your plans and ideas contribute in deriving a design?

The creative process is considerably complex. It goes through several phases and can be inspired by other domains outside architecture. During this exercise, copious written texts, drawings, models, sketches, renders, and other media are produced revolving around the idea that originated the project itself. Ideas generated during this process can be reused, or give rise to new ideas, or be set aside only to become relevant during another phase, or even lay dormant. This project is a great example of how an apparently simple architectural concept results in five distinct houses because the original intention, due to its flexibility, was the exploration of how formal similarity and difference can be studied and applied in different ways across the project.

How do you try to understand your clients' intentions?

Doubt is always one major issue we have to deal with when we receive a project commission, even when the client's intention appears clear and straightforward. It is our job to understand those doubts and desires, and explore the project's possibilities and limitations in order to answer the problems posed by the client and the program.

Top-floor plan

Second-floor plan

First-floor plan

How do you incorporate your client's proposals into your design schemes?

Schemes are a tool to communicate and solve problems created by requests or proposals. It is imperative to understand what role the client will take on during project development. Will they actively participate from the start? Do they have a predefined idea of what they want? Will they allow the design team to explore and allow the program to take the project wherever it may lead? The scheme serves

as a bridge between the client and architect for transmitting information about the project according to each one's level of involvement, doubling as a trust-building exercise toward the goal of realizing the project.

How do you make evaluations and judgments on your own schemes?
We believe that this particular project speaks for itself. It results from an evaluative concept applied in five different ways. Its coordination and the team's effort led to a greatly

satisfying creation, for both the client and the team which
conceived it. An architect should be capable of constantly
questioning their own work, as well as allowing it to be
questioned by others during the entire design process. The
importance of being a part of a team is that it facilitates this
necessity by building into the process external, internal, and
cross-disciplinary criticism.

How do you stay curious in complex and disordered situations?

A conceptual idea feeds itself with questions. The same
happens with a project during the design process. While
seeking answers, constant research and updating is required
at every step, enabling and injecting creativity in its full
potential. Curiously, this not only enriches current projects
in development and future projects that come to be, it also
helps refine and improve overall methods and procedures. The
Areia project reached a level of synthesis in its complexity that
unified the team's way of thinking such that it even motivated
the client's curiosity and helped him organize his own ideas.

When designing, not all of an architect's ideas can always be fully realized. Could you share on how to handle such a situation?

A conceptual idea at the start, being nothing more than a scheme or diagram, is devoid of design. Only when it is formalized by sketches or drawings does design begin to enter. Ideas, when they have inherent quality, can be recorded for later use, recycled, reused, adapted, inverted, and can even give birth to new ideas. In Areia, there was the opportunity to implement this process, right at the earliest stage of conception, and it became part of the strategy that defined this project. Ideas should never be discarded or forgotten, since sometimes, all they need to be successful is finding their correct place in time.

When you worked on this project, how did you strive to maintain your original idea from beginning to end?

The Areia project began with a clear idea of mutating flexibility, so that it responds to the program needs; schemes and drawings seek to find solutions. Many things may occur during the conception of the project that deviate from or question the original project intentions. Therefore, an intervention strategy was developed to, given our past experience, withstand controlled deviations that were foreseen. We believe that design needs to have the ability to respond and adapt in order to achieve the overarching concept that guides the project.

How do you make a comprehensive judgment on a design's progress and optimize the process?

Optimization is directly connected with productivity and scheduling. It represents a chance to make time, to produce intellectual work, and to navigate through creative new ideas. It also means that it becomes possible to review and reanalyze important decisions and think objectively about the next ones.

How do you identify critical problems and seek solutions?

During every project's development, a series of questions are raised (though not necessarily at the same time), which

require certain skills to overcome. This process implies
that the answers stem from recognizing that the problem
exists. The definition of the questions and the openness to
embrace the challenge of the answers may lead the project.
On this project, the primal idea that defined the project was
able to solve not only design issues, but technical problems
as well. It was able to withstand structural and technical
infrastructural maneuvers without compromising the built
reflection of the conceptual idea.

**What role does teamwork play in identifying problems that may have
been overlooked?**

Communication is a matter of great interest for everyone
involved in an architecture project. The origin of creativity and
the project's originality lie in each individual's participation
in the design process. As architects, we have an additional
responsibility to coordinate and assist the other disciplines in
their contribution toward this common goal.

**How do you respond to unexpected problems that occur during the
design process?**

It is usually when we think that a design process has no
problems, or that we have answered all the design questions,
that new and unpredictable issues arise. These represent
an important part of design development and should be
embraced as a positive element in the project's evolution.
We have encountered unexpected design problems in Areia,
mostly caused by structural issues, as some elements
were added at the last minute and needed to be fused with
the whole set. In this situation, we conscientiously opted
to assume them as a natural part of the architectural
composition, and maintained our position in stating that none
of those options compromised the project itself. It is our duty
and privilege as architects to think creatively and seek the
appropriate solutions.

"We always break down complex things to their ground. It is astonishing how well this works."

Schiller Architektur BDA

Patrick Schiller founded Schiller Architektur BDA in 2003. Schiller graduated from HFT Stuttgart in 2000 and worked in various practices before establishing his own studio, taking over the projects and employees of his father's former office, Manfred Schiller. After winning several awards for single-family residences, Schiller Architektur BDA shifted focus to multi-residential housing. In 2010, the practice added commercial buildings to its portfolio, as well as project development. Schiller was appointed to Bund Deutscher Architekten (BDA) in 2012.

PROJECT NAME---DA08 supermarket
LOCATION---Wangen im Allgäu, Germany
COMPLETED---2012
AREA---26,910 square feet (2,500 square meters)
DESIGN---Schiller Architektur BDA
PHOTOGRAPHY---Brigida González

The DA08 supermarket was designed to consume as little energy as possible, in both its production and operation. Weekly markets and market halls served as inspiration for the building and lighting concept.

The form of the building is made of alternating high and low volumes that combine with polycarbonate panels to introduce daylight into the building and create a comfortable environment. The shell of the building offers excellent thermal insulation and ensures a constant climate to help keep the building and goods cool. The alternating ceiling height

creates a favorable temperature layering where warm exhaust air escapes through the skylights and cool air is supplied from below.

While much of the building is made of vertical forms, the entrance has a long, white horizontal profile that extends a covered area outside. The café, bakery, fresh produce, and checkout zones are located near the entrance area. The café terrace opens to a beautiful view of the Swabian Alp and fruit trees, and the bakery features a drive-in. Shelving is stacked to a maximum height of 5.25 feet (1.6 meters) and kept deliberately low to provide customers with a good overview of the market. Skylights significantly reduce electricity consumption; the daylight also provides a much wider color spectrum than traditional lighting, creating a pleasant and natural atmosphere for shopping.

The structural materials, including half-timbered girders, rolled steel profiles, and bolted steel cassettes were selected for their economy, recyclability, dismantlability, and low energy consumption during manufacture. The materials also reduced construction time to six months. The skylights and western part of the flat roof were additionally equipped with a photovoltaic system.

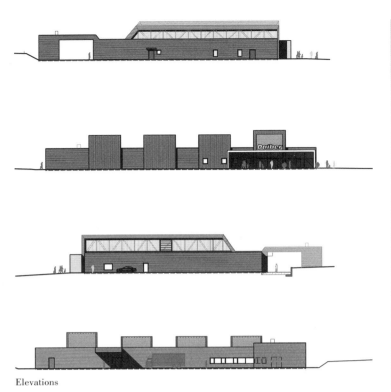

Elevations

How do you resolve the unfavorable aspects of site conditions?

The site is the most important element of a building, and our buildings always reflect the conditions of the site. We don't see it as unfavorable factors; they help us to design the structure and to work on the building as a reflection of the site and the wishes of the builder. We have a lot of countryside around the DA08 supermarket, so we tried to keep the building profile flat and used a dark color to make it fit into the fields and the woods. The skylights, which give form to the roof and to the whole building, are aligned north–south and this is the main factor of the site, in a broader sense.

How do you put forward solutions comprehensively and objectively without any prejudgments?

Usually, we start every project from zero. We analyze the site, program of the builder, local building rules, and so on. With all of these factors in mind, we work curiously on the project, excited at what it will be like. It is a floating, totally logical process, so there is no room for prejudgments in our work. At the end, you have programmatic rooms with all of their requirements and you need to find a structure that fits the rooms and requirements. In the case of the supermarket, we wanted to build a market hall flooded with daylight to make customers feel good. This increases the attraction of the market in comparison to its competitors that have similar products with similar prices.

How do you perceive the abstract architectural space?

Space, function, and light are the most important elements of our work. Usually, you just see space and light, so these are the primary elements that touch the senses. Within the supermarket, we wanted to create the mood of a market or a market hall. High rooms with natural daylight make you feel good and support the presentation of merchandise. As most supermarkets have similar goods and prices, people go shopping in places that make them feel good, and if you're in a good mood you buy more. It's a staged seduction.

How do you coordinate the relationship between function, space, style, and circulation?

We concentrate on function and space because these are the things that stay. We usually don't care about "styles." We develop the building logically and often the style is limited economically. The supermarket had to fit an economical concept and an ecological wish from the builder and in so doing, turned out as a low-cost, long-lasting construction made of wood and steel. It has low upkeep and doesn't use much energy, and can be recycled; at the end of the day, we have a very structured façade fitting our building perfectly.

How do your plans and ideas contribute in deriving a design?

As commercial construction projects are often designed in close cooperation with the clients, there's often a back-and-forth with ideas concerning workflow and benefits for the users/clients. In the case of the supermarket project, we radically changed the layout three times to optimize the workflow for the employees and to improve the shopping experience for the customers. For example, the delivery and refuse collection areas were changed several times to guarantee the shortest, smoothest route possible to and fro. In relation to customer experience, the drinks vending area was changed several times and eventually, a beverage cold room was created out of a pool of ideas that was built by earlier planning concepts. Ultimately, in every project, there is always a pool of previous ideas which may be declined or reused in the next step.

How do you try to understand your clients' intentions?

One of the most important projects we take on is to build houses for our clients, so we need to be empathic and try our best to realize and optimize their wishes. Often, it is akin to a detective game. You need to make your clients think about the functions and possibilities of a building much more than they did before. You need to give them hints so they can sometimes find hidden wishes, or maybe reduce them and go back to the basics.

How do you incorporate your client's proposals into your design schemes?

As mentioned before, we are sensitive to the client's wishes and break them down to the basics. We question why they want things in order to help them think about their needs. After that, we start to develop functional schemes and patterns, and in the process of our work transform them into spaces.

How do you make evaluations and judgments on your own schemes?

It is the part of other people to judge our works and schemes.
We reflect on our finished project and learn from them
by keeping in contact with our clients. In the case of the
supermarket, we had some small changes within the furniture
that showed us things about the movements of the clients.

How do you stay curious in complex and disordered situations?

Usually, we discuss such situations within our team, or with
the other engineers to find solutions. Many times, we need
to go some steps back and break things down to their roots.
We don't usually have problems staying curious as this is
the most beautiful part of our job. Often, we use music; it
is inspiring and brings energy, and sometimes the mood
influences the design.

**When designing, not all of an architect's ideas can always be fully
realized. Could you share on how to handle such a situation?**

There are many examples in architecture history, as well as
is in the history of our office, when an effective design cannot
be implemented but is still promising. Some ideas end up
being realized years later with more experience. Because

of this, never lose your ideas as sometimes, these dreams come true. This is what keeps us creative.

When you worked on this project, how did you strive to maintain your original idea from beginning to end?

We usually don't have problems maintaining an idea from beginning to end as we don't have a starting idea per se; the idea develops within the design process. Once the idea is developed, we try to make it as succinct and consequent as possible. As we usually work in a minimalistic process, this is an important part of our work and we are aware of this.

How do you make a comprehensive judgment on a design's progress and optimize the process?

We don't think a design process should be optimized—you lose a lot then. Of course, you should avoid mistakes of the past. We optimize our office in many ways, but optimization of the design process will kill curiosity and the strange ideas that can lead to surprising results. We changed the floor plan of the supermarket three times to optimize the workflow. This was ineffective for us, but very effective for the client.

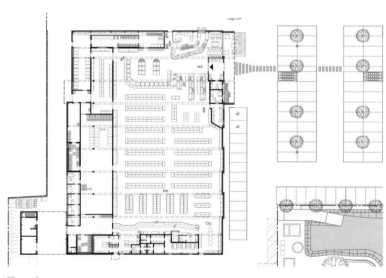

Floor plan

How do you identify critical problems and seek solutions?

        They're identified in the design process. We don't see them as problems, they're more challenges that need to be solved. When they appear, we discuss them with all the involved persons, such as engineers, clients, or even local authorities. In the DA08 project for instance, we had huge problems with the approval; it took over two years to get the permission, but we were able to realize the original idea.

What role does teamwork play in identifying problems that may have been overlooked?

        Teamwork is the base of our work. Other people have other perspectives and they see things differently, which translates to the collective of everyone, in turn, seeing more of the many facets. So it is usual in our office to check the work of other team members and share experiences and knowledge.

How do you respond to unexpected problems that occur during the design process?

Unexpected problems in a design process are mainly solved as an entire team, but not just within our staff. Clients and engineers are involved too. In the design process of the supermarket, there was very close teamwork between the client and our office, so unexpected problems were solved very fast.

"People are the greatest capital—a deep resource of ideas and energy."

Dinko Peračić, Roman Šilje

Dinko Peračić earned his master's degree at IAAC in Barcelona, Spain, and graduated from the University of Zagreb's Faculty of Architecture. Peračić is the founder of the architecture collective Platforma 9.81, and a partner in the architecture firm ARP. He has been working as an assistant at the Faculty of Civil Engineering, Architecture and Geodesy at the University of Split since 2008, and became an associate professor in the architectural design department in 2016.

Roman Šilje graduated from IAAC in Barcelona and the Faculty of Architecture at the University of Zagreb in Croatia. Since 2007, Šilje has been leading the architectural studio NORMALA in Zagreb. He worked as an assistant at Zagreb's Faculty of Architecture from 2006 to 2009 and was head of the UHA (Congress of Croatian Architects) Publishing Council from 2010 to 2012.

Peračić and Šilje designed the building for the Faculty of Civil Engineering at the University of Osijek, which was awarded the Medal of Architecture by the Croatian Chamber of Architects as the most important architectural creation in 2016.

PROJECT NAME---Faculty of Civil Engineering, University of Osijek
LOCATION---Osijek, Croatia
COMPLETED---2016
AREA---114,097 square feet (10,600 square meters)
DESIGN---Dinko Peračić, Roman Šilje
PHOTOGRAPHY---Damir Žižić

The Faculty of Civil Engineering in Osijek (GFOS) is a built-in within a complex of planned buildings. It is opened on its shorter sides and the longer façades face neighboring buildings with narrow and tall intermediate space in between. The cross section is profiled in order to bring natural light and air into the building. A narrow passage in the west expands to connect to the hall and portico with larger stay-zones. Slanting the façade in the east delivers more light into the classrooms and lecture rooms. Internal terraces and skylights open up the middle section of the building and provide places for informal interaction,

learning, and work. Natural light reaches down to the first floor, and air circulates into the middle part of the building.

The longitudinal section highlights the importance of communication spaces in contemporary education, providing places for individual and group work, meetings, and small and large events. The building is passable from the basement to the top floor by way of wide circulation spaces that have various functions, such as open classrooms, a canteen, grandstands, terraces, porticos, offices, and lobbies.

All corridors have open ends, which emphasize the transparent character of the building and bring additional light inside. Bearing constructions, consisting of five continuous perforated walls executed in visible reinforced-concrete, put stress on the basic cross profile of the building and emphasize the long open corridors. As a primary space-shaping element, they are perforated to create necessary cross connections, passages, light breakthroughs, visual contacts, and consolidated spaces. Movement through the building represents a cinematographic experience with a number of sequential spaces connected by character and light.

How do you resolve the unfavorable aspects of site conditions?

An important part of almost every piece of architecture is its location in space and time. It often offers an array of questions that we are supposed to read carefully, choosing the most important ones to address. It is crucial to define—even verbalize—or draw the biggest questions. A creative architectural answer to well-defined questions about the context gives sense to architecture. We need to be hungry for problems and constraints. The more of them you can absorb, process, and turn into creations, the richer the architecture will be.

The Faculty of Civil Engineering had to be placed in the middle of a large empty plot within a very dense structural plan. This illogical condition provoked a search for an architectural answer that presented the new structure like an interpolation, or even an interior project, rather than a self-standing building.

How do you put forward solutions comprehensively and objectively without any prejudgments?

Architecture depends on unpredictable imagination and unexpected answers. These cannot come out of the bare analysis and pure distillation of facts. Wrong lines, mistakes,

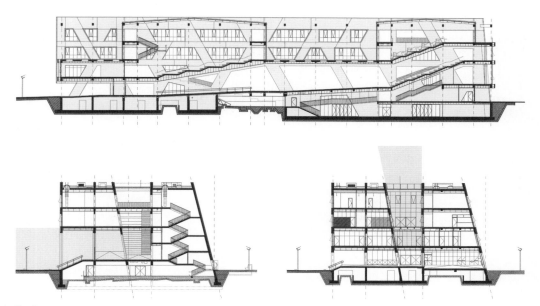

Sections

irrational decisions, brave experiments, and other wild ideas push it forward. Of course, it can be full of self-oriented fascinations, conceptual dead-ends, and irrelevant outcomes. One needs to be honest enough to make a severe reality check on their ideas and brave enough to strongly push forward the ones that survive such a test.

We are interested in the meaning and message of architecture. In the case of GFOS, we wanted to provide a new energetic and dynamic spirit to the institution in a not-so-optimistic transitional context. It intentionally doesn't respond to actual circumstances, but tries to encourage the ambitions of students and scientific staff.

How do you perceive the abstract architectural space?

Visiting GFOS is definitively not a photographic experience. It is more a cinematographic one. We had a problem making photographs that could represent it properly. It is designed through movements and only by walking through can one experience its spaces to the full potential.

Architecture should be seen as a time-based art. It is a chain of sequences, a ceremony of experiences, and a discovery game played by movement through its structure. Instagram-friendly architecture based on one perfect exterior or interior image is a betrayal to the people who come to use it.

How do you coordinate the relationship between function, space, style, and circulation?

Synthesis is the key skill of an architect. We should teach, train, and learn it in more detail because it could remain our only distinctive element in the crowd of specialists and experts who master their narrow subjects. Contrary to the trends, we should remain generalists, capable of processing diverse information, using knowledge and skills of different disciplines to create an answer in space. Orchestrating functions, forms, styles, and circulations is a mere minimum. There are more ingredients to be added to the formula, such as program, budget, context, usage, and so on.

An important reason why our GFOS proposal was selected in the competition was the addition of extra spaces for informal learning and gathering between lecture rooms, studios, and offices that were not defined in the brief. Our main concern was to shape a quality learning environment by balancing the elements of the built structure.

Fourth-floor plan

Third-floor plan

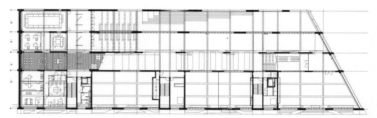

Second-floor plan

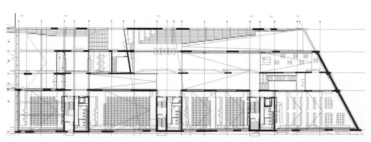

First-floor plan

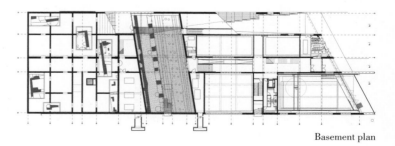

Basement plan

How do your plans and ideas contribute in deriving a design?

An idea is much more valuable when it takes shape. Words are important in architecture, but it is accelerated when they are transferred into drawings. A picture is worth a thousand words and sometimes, one drawing provokes the other. It is fun to play with drawings that sometimes keep in line with and sometimes escape from each other. While preparing the proposal for GFOS, we communicated by drawings, putting one on top of the other, constantly raising the complexity and choosing the elements of order.

How do you try to understand your clients' intentions?

People build architecture. Of course, we need to understand and manipulate their intentions.

How do you incorporate your client's proposals into your design schemes?

It depends on the client and we need to find out their proposals early in the design process. Some people expect the architect to take care of it all and some want to be more hands-on throughout the process. We prefer when people see it as their project and when they are involved. We like to develop the dweller and the house together.

How do you make evaluations and judgments on your own schemes?

The most efficient way to check the ideas is to present them to friends or someone independent whom you trust. It is useful, even for the ideas that you are sure about.

How do you stay curious in complex and disordered situations?

Architects need problems to make them into creations. It is not always easy, but complex situations, when processed and distilled into questions, often require and enable creative solutions. A crisis is always potential for something new.

When designing, not all of an architect's ideas can always be fully realized. Could you share on how to handle such a situation?

An architectural project can be made out of a few design decisions. It is not wise to put in every productive concept that appears along the way. Ideas mutate, transform, adapt, and transfer through projects. Once they appear, they are never fully dismissed. Sometimes, it takes decades to find their place, mostly in some new shape.

When you worked on this project, how did you strive to maintain your original idea from beginning to end?

Designs evolve through their processes. Some steps might be destructive and can erase or fade the core concept. We should look for the other ones that enforce and develop their values.

How do you make a comprehensive judgment on a design's progress and optimize the process?

The design process is a joy and we should enjoy while we create. The production parts are to be optimized as much as possible, allowing enough time and stimulating environments for the creative parts. Optimization serves to make free time for creation.

How do you identify critical problems and seek solutions?

We should be hungry for problems and questions. The definition of a proper question, put in an inspiring way, is halfway to the solution.

What role does teamwork play in identifying problems that may have been overlooked?

People are the greatest capital—a deep resource of ideas and energy. In one way or another, our works depend on people. An important skill of architects is to orchestrate people involved in the projects, making space for much individual creativeness and many contributions.

How do you respond to unexpected problems that occur during the design process?

To remain elastic in critical situations and have a processing power to face unpredictable problems is a very useful skill for an architect. We should see problems as benefits to the project, as long as we are capable of conceiving the creative answers and turning them into new layers of value.

"The project should have a main idea. That idea should have a reason."

Kurtul Erkmen

Kurtul Erkmen founded KG Mimarlık in 1990. Erkmen graduated as a master architect from the Istanbul State Academy of Fine Arts, now known as Mimar Sinan Fine Arts University, in 1983. He teaches architecture at the Istanbul State Academy; is a cofounder of Aura Istanbul; is a jury member in architecture competitions; and a regular speaker at conferences and seminars.

KG Mimarlık is an award-winning architecture practice active in interior design and architecture in Turkey. The studio also undertakes projects in Russia, Romania, Saudi Arabia, Libya, Congo, Kazakhstan, Turkmenistan, and Uzbekistan.

PROJECT NAME---Deposite building
LOCATION---Istanbul, Turkey
COMPLETED---2017
AREA---37,728 square feet (3,505 square meters)
DESIGN---KG Mimarlık
PHOTOGRAPHY---Büşra Yeltekin

The Deposite building is located in Istanbul's Ikitelli Organized Industrial Zone. The new warehouse building with vehicular access is adjacent to an existing office building; a new upper floor has been added to the office building to function as a mosque that can hold around 520 people.

The new warehouse building and the new upper floor are unified through the same architectural language—metal cladding. Two ramps provide vehicle entry and exit from the front and rear for the transportation of goods to and from the warehouse.

The metal cladding on the new buildings is punctured with a graphical pattern composed of square and rectangular windows that bring daylight inside. The bright yellow frames contrast with the dark gray metal and complement the residential buildings opposite.

How do you resolve the unfavorable aspects of site conditions?

Analyze the data that will affect your project, such as land conditions, construction rights, architectural program, and client expectations. Most of the time they contradict, thus locating and identifying problems are key to starting correctly. Land conditions and construction rights are fixed, but the architectural program and client expectations may vary. You can insist on such changes if you find it necessary. In our Deposite project, we made a lot of effort to combine the new upper floor of the existing building and the new warehouse building into a single form.

Elevation

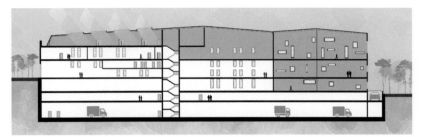

Section

How do you put forward solutions comprehensively and objectively without any prejudgments?

Think about which solution will answer all the data. Don't settle for the first solution that comes to mind, even though it usually ends up being the most accurate one. The solutions don't need to be prejudice-free; I would even argue that they cannot be. To a certain extent, the entire project experience, background and emotional state of the architects are channelled into every design they create. This subjectivity turns architecture into a form where art and engineering are mixed together.

How do you perceive the abstract architectural space?

Look for different alternatives and make a choice. It might be tiring, but at least you won't be thinking: "Could it be better?" Paul Rudolph said, "I try every alternate, even the ones that don't come to my mind." The mosque located on the top floor of the existing building in Deposite was originally planned in a different location by the client. Taking into account the potential of the top floor, as it receives light from above instead of the façade, we proposed relocating the *masjid* and got approval.

How do you coordinate the relationship between function, space, style, and circulation?

When the circulation is well organized, all that remains are the spaces. The relationship between this pair shows how function has been interpreted. Therefore, all the spaces that are configured and expected to be used in accordance with the main function are actually a result of the transportation-space relationship. And in that, the resolved task of function is transformed into a project. The style that is expected to come into play at this point is reflected in the design as a means of the architect's own inner world, their style of creation, and what they want to see or show.

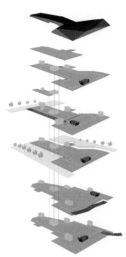

Axonometric diagram

How do your plans and ideas contribute in deriving a design?

For me, the idea is the beginning. Design follows the idea, after which come the plans. What is put on paper in terms of plan, cross section, elevation, and details are actually the means of representing the design of an idea that was initially abstract. So, let's ask this, "Are plans devoid of an 'idea,' architecturally?" To me, absolutely not!

How do you try to understand your clients' intentions?

In general, the time architects need, and the time clients can provide are inversely proportional. Time limitations should not scare you. Sometimes limited time creates an opportunity to show your creativity. Don't forget, performance equals work/time. There is worse for us who complain about the lack of time—and that is infinite time. Unending projects can be terribly tiring. Console yourself with this thought.

How do you incorporate your client's proposals into your design schemes?

The project should have a main idea. That idea should have a reason. What we call the design's "essence" is hidden here. Sometimes, it resurfaces, as in Eero Saarinen's TWA Flight Center and Peter Zumthor's Bruder Klaus Field Chapel. Our desire to treat Deposite's roof and façade as one shell made us search for a suitable material. Thus, the idea of moving a material that is appropriate for the roof to the façade was the best solution and we enveloped the building with a shell by choosing a metal cover.

How do you make evaluations and judgments on your own schemes?

Sometimes, the concept might seem impracticable. Don't worry about it. The hardest or most impossible-looking ideas have been made possible with creative solutions. Technology and engineering are at your service. You can consult.

How do you stay curious in complex and disordered situations?

The process to turn the concept into something practicable might require a lot of work. It's as if everything starts over. If you are sure of your idea, don't give up on it easily. Remember. if you want an easy solution and to work less, it means settling with a clichéd, trite project. But our job is producing creative, new, and fresh solutions. At one stage of this project, the client wanted vehicle entry and we had to come up with a solution that involved two different paths on suitable floors.

When designing, not all of an architect's ideas can always be fully realized. Could you share on how to handle such a situation?

Right at the outset, there are some differences between a design that will remain on paper and a design that will actually be implemented, built, dwelt in, and used. The second one does not result solely on the competence of the architectural solution. It endeavours to manage a multi-layered structure such as legal restrictions, economy, technology, and the client's priorities in the best possible way. The balance between concessions that can be made and those that will not be accepted determines the final product. What was "unrealized," in the Deposite project was, in fact, the "unable" that occurred during the implementation phase, not the project. Because the reason is economical, the architect can't do much, other than not get too attached to some parts.

When you worked on this project, how did you strive to maintain your original idea from beginning to end?

Seeking and finding a way to reconcile all factors and satisfy everyone involved who has a say in the design and construction is already part of the implementation of the original idea. When you lose your strength to concentrate, pause and do something else, even if it's for a short time. Clear your mind, take a walk, or watch a movie. Do something else because there are many examples of times like this when you will suddenly and unexpectedly arrive at the answer needed as the subconscious keeps working. I think it is best for the architect to withdraw from the project if the idea is diluted, blurred out of its roots, or when there isn't even an idea left to defend.

How do you make a comprehensive judgment on a design's progress and optimize the process?

The design process requires resisting various difficulties and overcoming obstacles. Some projects are easier and some are more difficult. Ignoring the ongoing search for the right solution of various sub-functions—which, here, were

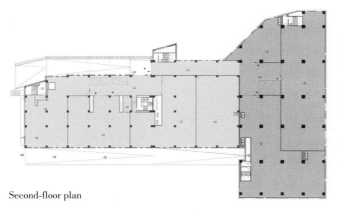

Second-floor plan

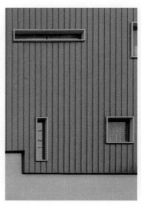

frequently relocated by the employer—helped; it was not a project that troubled me.

How do you identify critical problems and seek solutions?

As you approach the end of the project, turn to the beginning and check that the idea and purpose determined in the beginning have not changed in the process. Sometimes, you can find yourself far from where you started. There is no problem if you're pleased with the result.

What role does teamwork play in identifying problems that may have been overlooked?

It is good to consult others, get ideas, or discuss the project while managing the process. Another eye might help surface a situation you had not noticed before. Listen to your team members. Sometimes, you will hear things that don't sit well with you, so be it. Maybe a different view can suddenly be mind-opening. The same goes with the experiences you will gather throughout your life. Oscar Niemeyer said, "What attracts me are free and sensual curves. The curves in my country's mountains; in the sinuous flow of its rivers; in the beloved woman's body."

How do you respond to unexpected problems that occur during the design process?

The most appropriate way to deal with an unpredictable problem is to be ready for it from the beginning. So mentally, if you know that there will often be unexpected problems, problems will not be unexpected. In fact, if you consider them as variable project input, they will cease to be "problems." Since the mission is to transform various data into a project (design), if you assume that the information given to you at the beginning may be incomplete, inaccurate, or flawed, it transforms the changes that will occur over time from "unpredictable" to "expected," and you will consider "the problem" simply as "new data."

"We believe in a totally flexible approach in terms of dealing with changes as they occur."

Blouin Orzes

Montréal-based Blouin Orzes architectes have been working in Nunavik, Québec, since 2000. Their projects include hotels and other residential, commercial, and institutional buildings in northern communities such as Kuujjuarapik, Puvirnituq, Salluit, and Kuujjuaq. Blouin Orzes also designed Polar Bears International House in Churchill, Manitoba.

With a sustained presence in Northern Canada, Blouin Orzes have acquired an intimate knowledge of the land, the people, their needs, and their values. Profoundly attached to the North, Marc Blouin and Catherine Orzes have developed their unique expertise in design and construction techniques for this region.

PROJECT NAME---Katittavik Centre
LOCATION---Kuujjuaraapik, Canada
COMPLETED---2017
AREA---7,319 square feet (680 square meters)
DESIGN---Blouin Orzes architectes
PHOTOGRAPHY---Blouin Orzes architectes

Katittavik Centre is located in the Northern Village of Kuujjuaraapik, near the mouth of the Great Whale River. The slightly lopsided one-and-a-half-story building seems to have been shaped by the strong winter winds. A light aerial structure signals the entrance portico, where people can linger and enjoy views of the river.

Openings are kept to a minimum given the hall's function, harsh climate conditions, and high energy costs. A well-lit lobby, adjacent to a small office area, leads to the large multipurpose space, which is the project's raison d'être. The unconventional ceiling height is intended to create a warm, welcoming feeling for community members. A small platform, serving as a control booth for sound, lighting, and projections floats above the hall. The backstage area is equipped with services, storage, and a small kitchen.

The center has retractable seating to accommodate up to 300 people. The main hall can be rearranged for banquets, performances, lectures, and film projections. State-of-the-art video conferencing equipment enables community members to be in contact with the rest of the world—a must for this geographically and linguistically isolated community.

Katittavik Centre is the first phase of a larger project that will integrate nearby St. Edmund's Anglican Church, Nunavik's oldest standing structure. The architects hope that the center, the church, and the adjacent public space will eventually form a significant cultural and civic pole.

How do you resolve the unfavorable aspects of site conditions?

The challenges encountered by our office are not so much related to the actual sites, but rather, to their remoteness in Nunavik's northern locations. Building materials and components are purchased in the southern part of Canada and can only be shipped during a very short summer season. Typically, a shipment will leave Montréal at the end of June and reach a destination such as Kuujjuaraapik a month later.

Another important challenge relates to weather conditions in the North and the need to provide workers with a protected environment as soon as possible. Our solution has been to use prefabricated elements, which can be rapidly assembled. Once the exterior shell is up, construction work can take place under satisfactory conditions.

How do you put forward solutions comprehensively and objectively without any prejudgments?

As architects who build for the Inuit people, we have to adapt to their cultural ways—very different from what we are accustomed to in southern locations. It usually takes years to build the necessary trust to engage in a satisfactory

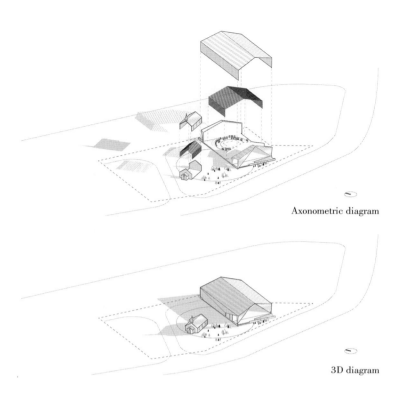

Axonometric diagram

3D diagram

working relationship. No decision is made without a lengthy consultation process and consensus has to be reached. Changes are also quite common as members of a community become more aware of a project. In the case of Katittavik, the original request was to host the traditional Inuit Games, a popular event among northern communities. The program expanded into a multifunctional hall, which meant more space, but also higher costs. Our team not only helped redefine the project but also got involved in finding additional sources of financing.

How do you perceive the abstract architectural space?

The structures that our team builds in the North are often very straightforward. We have already completed a number of small hotels, as well as municipal, cultural, and industrial buildings. Contrary to architects working in dense urban contexts, we often build on open land. Movements in and out

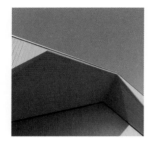

of buildings are dictated by weather conditions, which can be extreme at times.

In Kuujjuaraapik, the close proximity to an existing nineteenth-century historical church was a major factor in the siting of the multipurpose hall. The eventual renovation of the church as an interpretation center helped create a new cultural pole as it shares a common exterior space with the center.

How do you coordinate the relationship between function, space, style, and circulation?

The transition from the outside to the inside takes on extreme importance for the Inuit people. Going from a cold environment to a warm interior usually occurs through a series of transitory porticoes. Symbolically, the journey from a public sphere to more intimate or private spaces is also significant. As we worked on the Katittavik project, we integrated these specific cultural elements by introducing a slightly elaborate entry sequence. It starts with a protected outdoor space, which then opens to an interior lobby. From there, one reaches the heart of the building—its warmest space, both physically and symbolically. The central hall is where community members and visitors congregate, communicate, and share.

How do your plans and ideas contribute in deriving a design?

When our office started working in Nunavik twenty years ago, we were asked to build a small hotel for professionals and

Elevations

visitors who needed accommodation when they visited for a few days. We developed a first prototype with a few rooms and a common living area, which doubled as a meeting room when needed. The plan was used a number of times over the years with slight improvements or variations to adapt to different sites or program. Given severe construction constraints and high costs, as well as the need to protect buildings from natural elements, volumes are compact, and openings are strategically located. In the case of Katittavik, the hall itself is practically windowless to ensure maximum protection from the cold and wind.

How do you try to understand your clients' intentions?

Our office is usually called in to work in Nunavik once a community has made a decision that there is a need for a new facility, or to upgrade an existing one. Our job is to accompany the community and its representatives through

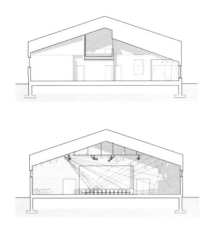

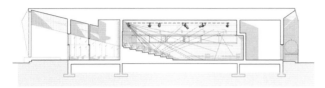

Sections

the process that will eventually result in a building. Thanks
to a climate of trust, which we have built over the last two
decades, we are able to explore possibilities or avenues
that can enrich a project, while keeping within reasonable
budgets. We believe in a totally flexible approach in terms
of dealing with changes as they occur. We are also willing to
get involved in the search for funding, which can sometimes
make a huge difference as far as budgets are concerned.

**How do you incorporate your client's proposals into your design
schemes?**

Once our clients have stated their programmatic intentions,
long discussions take place until we fully understand their
needs. Some of the wishes expressed on these occasions
deal with minor points, such as the color of the exterior
siding. Other requests are much more significant to the
community, such as the integration of a particular object or

art piece. Agreeing to these requests is often not that crucial for the professionals, but it means a lot to the concerned community members who can then feel that they have had a true impact on a given project.

How do you make evaluations and judgments on your own schemes?

Every time we tackle a project, we make a deliberate effort, in terms of design, and resisting the transferring our southern reflexes to northern situations. We try to constantly remain aware of each project's specific geographical and cultural context. We strongly believe that this constant questioning on our part will help future users fully identify with their new facility.

How do you stay curious in complex and disordered situations?

Public consultations are an essential component of the process, which leads to the development of numerous projects. It allows us to not just meet with the decision makers, but also with the locals who are the future users of a particular facility. Discussions are often disorderly and at times, openly critical toward community leaders, but they can also lead to unusual remarks. These may seem out of context at the time, but somehow they linger in our memory until we finally understand what they mean. The outcome of great wisdom—these observations sometimes guide us toward new architectural avenues—is unexpected yet promising.

When designing, not all of an architect's ideas can always be fully realized. Could you share on how to handle such a situation?

Every time we work on a project, there are always unexpected issues that come up. The knowledge we gain from this does not always apply to the project at hand, either because it is too late in the process or because it is not relevant. We take note, however, and look for opportunities to use this information, which helps us better respond to the context.

When you worked on this project, how did you strive to maintain your original idea from beginning to end?

As architects, our role is to help our clients answer their needs and reach their goals. We do believe in the importance of good design, but we also try to stay pragmatic when faced with issues such as remoteness, low budgets, or having to use non-descript existing structures to do a retrofit project. We never give up.

How do you make a comprehensive judgment on a design's progress and optimize the process?

There are many technical aspects to take into account when building in northern communities. With climate changes affecting polar regions even more severely than the South, new challenges have to be faced and a variety of solutions must be developed. The gradual melting of the permafrost layer requires architects to use extreme care when they choose sites for buildings or when figuring out the details of foundations. We have to learn from trial and error as we try to adapt to the major changes awaiting us.

How do you identify critical problems and seek solutions?

One of the critical problems we encounter when building in the North has been the lack of local workers with the skills we need. One of the solutions has been training people locally, but we are also relying heavily on prefabrication techniques. Building in Nunavik means the contractor selected for a project must be able to fully understand the architects' intentions and translate them into a building.

To facilitate the building and site supervision process, simple 3D models are generated to facilitate the understanding of how the project has to be put together. Prefabrication helps speed up the building process—an important aspect of building in the North where workers have to be protected from the cold as soon as possible.

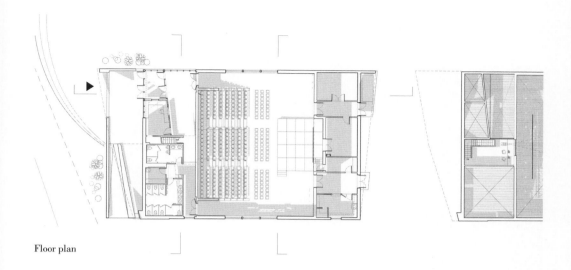

Floor plan

What role does teamwork play in identifying problems that may have been overlooked?

> The Inuit people lived as nomads and had no building tradition comparable to the traditions of the Western world for thousands of years. Despite this, however, professionals and community members are able to have real discussions on questions of architecture and construction. Once a building is up, it truly represents the outcome of close collaboration and teamwork.

How do you respond to unexpected problems that occur during the design process?

> The most common problems that can occur when building in the North are related to missing materials or components due to a delivery mistake. This is the type of situation that has made us intensely aware of the Inuit people's amazing resilience and resourcefulness. Using recycled materials or available parts, they come up with temporary solutions that can at times become permanent. This motivates us, as architects, to look for new approaches based on recycling and simpler details.

"An architectural project can be seen as a solution for a set of requirements inscribed on a set of circumstances."

Tiago do Vale

Tiago do Vale, founder of Tiago do Vale Arquitectos, studied architecture at the University of Coimbra in Portugal and has a postgraduate degree in Advanced Studies in Architectural Heritage from the University of Porto. He was a Senator at the University of Coimbra and a member of the University Assembly. Do Vale writes articles and monthly columns for prestigious Portuguese and international print publications. He also curates architectural events, such as Urban Dialogues, International Architecture Congress in 2014 and Mesturas, International Architecture Encounters Galicia-Portugal in Spain and Portugal from 2014 to 2019.

PROJECT NAME---Gafarim House
LOCATION---Ponte de Lima, Portugal
COMPLETED---2016
AREA---2,949 square feet (274 square meters)
DESIGN---Tiago do Vale Arquitectos
PHOTOGRAPHY---João Morgado

Garafim House has a tense dialogue between vernacular principles and a more abstract understanding of form, place, and landscape. In the context of a naturally fragmented and disconnected environment, Gafarim House offers a monolithic, opaque volume to the street, referencing the parallelepiped and massive volumes of northern Portuguese architecture, and adjusting that to the surrounding scale.

The entrance is a long transitional space that connects the exterior to the interior. From opaque to transparent, from shadow to light, this progressive contrast represents the duplicities and contradictions of

the design concept. From the compressed entrance, the space expands to a double-height volume that houses the open-plan kitchen, and dining and living room, citing the domestic organization of the region's vernacular homes.

A generous glass wall offers views of the property and Minho beyond. Natural light is moderated through the northeast openings and it animates the architecture throughout the day and year. The private rooms of the house develop without any explicit separation, with all bedrooms facing southeast. A small interior patio serves both the main bedroom and the bathrooms, and allows for the creation of a space that is formally inside of the house, but symbolically apart.

With vernacular and contemporary references, Gafarim House is a project about contradiction, opposition, and provocation, condensed in a simple, pragmatic structure.

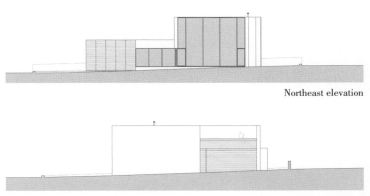

Northeast elevation

Northwest elevation

How do you resolve the unfavorable aspects of site conditions?

An architectural project can be seen as a solution for a set of requirements, inscribed on a set of circumstances. Though both the requirements and the circumstances could be seen as limiting (and unfavorable) factors to the full expression of an architectural object, the truth is that these conditioning elements are what shapes the architecture. They are the theme and the guiding line for the solution; one couldn't exist without the other. They are not a trap; they are the fuel.

In the case of Gafarim House, the site presented a street facing the sunlight, while expansive views faced north, inverting what we would usually seek. Embracing the circumstances produced a project that is opaque and mysterious to the street, while taking the opportunity to open itself extensively to the landscape in a way that would be impractical to do if facing south and the direct sunlight.

How do you put forward solutions comprehensively and objectively without any prejudgments?

Architectural design is an exercise of great complexity. To find a good solution, we must both rationalize the problem and risk intuitive jumps in a very demanding balance. But an

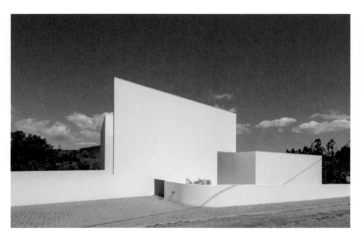

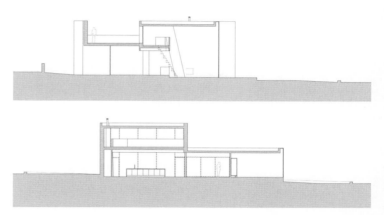

Sections

efficient architectural process should always progress from the most general questions toward the particulars.

Neither a detail should be set before understanding the global aspects of a project, nor any particular option be excluded before the general strategic options are mastered.

How do you perceive the abstract architectural space?

Architecture isn't a static art. Though generally, a building doesn't move, we move through it, and with the movement comes a sequence of spatial experiences. That sequence—the "architectural promenade," as Le Corbusier famously coined it—should be an object of design with as much fervor as the shape of the walls because the true experience of architecture is invariably dynamic.

We approached the Gafarim House entrance sequence that way. It begins with a blind façade that only communicates its entrance point. As we approach the door, the space compresses under a lower roof, creating a place of transition that expands to the interior when crossing the door. At the end of the entrance movement, the space finally decompresses to a double-height and fully transparent area, relishing that sensorial contrast.

How do you coordinate the relationship between function, space, style, and circulation?

Architecture is a balancing act. Most of the time, the work of the architect isn't about providing an answer that solves all, but finding the answer that presents the best balance between the performance of the building and the price one has to pay for it. It is about finding the best compromise between all the moving parts, all the circumstances, and all the demands. For that, one has to have a strong grasp of the nature of all these parts and how they relate to each other.

In this project, the most demanding compromises were in the balance between natural light and the site characteristics, and the balance between transparency and privacy.

How do your plans and ideas contribute in deriving a design?

Sometimes, certain solutions are motivated by latent interests of the office, theoretical beliefs, and pre-existent schemes—forces that exist prior to the project (and outside of it) and which will shape it. In the Gafarim House project, because the challenges were slightly unusual, the solution came directly from the requirements of the project and the circumstances of its place. The Gafarim House was informed, of course, by all the ideas and plans we always have lingering in our minds, but what generated its design came entirely from its own starting point and from its process.

How do you try to understand your clients' intentions?

The starting point for a project has to be the client's requirements. Different clients have a different grasp of the possibilities and of the implications and consequences of each option. So, even if the requirements are to be taken literally sometimes, it is also possible that they have to be interpreted to determine the reasons behind them and find a program that answers those reasons in the best way possible. As it frequently happens with residential architecture, the clients' intentions are quite standard. The challenge in this project was to adapt those intentions to a plot that had a non-standard relationship with the sunlight, the views, and the street.

How do you incorporate your client's proposals into your design schemes?

Our aim in architecture is to always simultaneously answer dozens of different questions and dozens of different problems with a single, simple gesture. That elegant, systematic approach will have positive implications for the development of the project and for the quality of the built work. But, of course, rarely such a broad stroke will hold up to scrutiny against the minute requirements of an architectural project and its client's demands. The process needs do happen the other way around. The beginning can't be a master stroke. It all has to

start from a deep understanding of the client's requests, of the possible compromises, and of the potential solutions that can be harmonized with them.

How do you make evaluations and judgments on your own schemes?

There may occasionally be a distance between the abstract strategies of a design and the concrete practicalities of the client's requests. Though the first aims to give an encompassing answer to the second, it is important to regularly evaluate that the commanding design principles don't compromise the pragmatic objectives of the design.

How do you stay curious in complex and disordered situations?

Chaos, disorder, and curiosity are central to informing the structured, systematic development process of a project. The process of Gafarim House was no different in that regard: we kept feeding on all sorts of sources that could provide new information, new stimuli, unexpected solutions, and provocations to our process, be it from, you name it, colleagues' work, from plastic arts, music, fashion, industrial design, poetry, and more. Without that flow of varied input, a design can become poorer or, worse, stagnant.

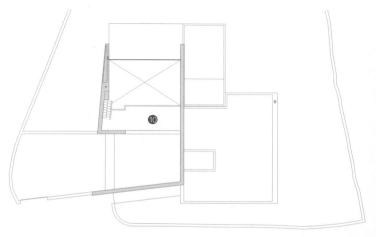

Mezzanine floor plan

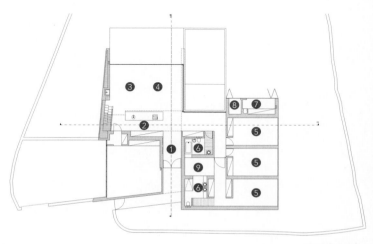

1 Entrance
2 Kitchen
3 Living room
4 Dining room
5 Bedroom
6 Bathroom
7 Outdoor kitchen
8 Mechanical room
9 Patio
10 Mezzanine

First-floor plan

When designing, not all of an architect's ideas can always be fully realized. Could you share on how to handle such a situation?

There's always a distance between abstract concept and built concept. Sometimes, the architect can be ambitious in trying to push the envelope to realize a certain vision, however, that can create friction with other pragmatic aspects of the development of a project, be it because of technical challenges or budgetary challenges.

We had faced such a moment during the design of Gafarim House with the glass façade that opens toward the landscape. We had aimed to design it with bigger glass panes and fewer divisions, which would have placed a lot of pressure on the costs and the structural demands of the solution. This generated the compromise seen on the final design.

Technical or budgetary constraints are legitimate project input and the resulting designs are genuine and truthful

solutions; they shouldn't be cast away as they are hallmarks of good architecture.

When you worked on this project, how did you strive to maintain your original idea from beginning to end?

We always work intensely—starting from the most general questions toward the more detailed particulars. For an idea to survive the entire process, we have to exhaust all possibilities and select the best possible option at each stage before progressing to the next.

With Gafarim House, we had to solve the program distribution and its relationship with the street and the sunlight, and the views. We didn't move to any other particulars before locking the ideal composition in the most general ways. This allowed us to be confident that no surprises would emerge as the project developed, to generate new data contributing to its design.

How do you make a comprehensive judgment on a design's progress and optimize the process?

The single most impactful aspect in the quality of architectural design is neither the individual capacities of the people involved, neither the choices of software used, nor the time and money a client has. The process is the most impactful thing in the quality of an architect's work. Systematizing base-work production, conceptual approaches, development stages, drawing standards, review systems, and detailing parameters can streamline the architectural process, make it more efficient, and facilitate higher and consistent quality standards. It is the foundation for a creative design to reach its highest potential.

How do you identify critical problems and seek solutions?

I find that, most of the time, the critical problems and their solutions are what will set the theme of the project. However,

one has to set the process in such a way that these are identified at the very first steps of the development of the project. If they come later, and if they truly are critical, they won't be properly solved without a full reconsideration of the design strategy, which will be both frustrating and costly. Identifying the critical aspects of a particular project is the first moment of our process, and we did the same with Gafarim House. At those moments, we have the entire office pour over the circumstances of the project and its requirements, and with different sets of eyes, skills and of sensitivities, we pinpoint the key challenges that will make or break the project and which need to be solved by it.

What role does teamwork play in identifying problems that may have been overlooked?

There is no replacement for teamwork in an architectural practice. Different sensibilities, different skills, and different eyes can generate a much richer and more complete approach to the process, review it more critically, and produce fitter responses.

How do you respond to unexpected problems that occur during the design process?

The identification of the critical aspects of the project are placed at the very beginning of the development process, precisely in order to minimize unexpected problems. If a problem arises at a later stage, we need to evaluate if its scope fits inside the flexibility of the solution we're working on. However, if it's a critical, central problem that the solution didn't contemplate, then that makes the solution the problem. We'd have to go back to the drawing board and start from scratch. The Gafarim House project didn't suffer from those sort of difficulties, though. Once the solution was generally fixed, its development progressed on a linear path.

"A strong and clear position is crucial to staying radical."

Jean-Pierre Dürig

Jean-Pierre Dürig, founder of DÜRIG AG, lives and works in Zürich, Switzerland, and Madrid, Spain. Dürig received his architecture diploma from ETH Zürich in 1985. Based on successful competitions, he opened his own practice in 1987 and ran a partnership with Philippe Rämi from 1990 to 2002. Dürig returned to solo practice in 2003. There has been a great emphasis on competitions, both national and international, throughout Dürig's career; all major built projects are the result of first-prize awards and his projects have been displayed in several exhibitions. Dürig has also served as a visiting lecturer at ETH Zürich and a guest professor at the Academy of Architecture at Università della Svizzera italiana.

PROJECT NAME---Löwenstrasse transit station
LOCATION---Zürich, Switzerland
COMPLETED---2014
AREA---371,237 square feet (33,560 square meters)
DESIGN---DÜRIG AG
PHOTOGRAPHY---Ruedi Walti, Basel

The new underground Löwenstrasse transit station forms the centerpiece of the cross-city rail link in Zürich. The four railway tracks and two platforms of this transit station are 52.5 feet (16 meters) underground, below tracks 4 to 9 of the upper central station. Above the platform is a new shopping level, stretching both east and west and interrupted by the river Sihl, which flows beneath the main station.

Straightforward and clearly arranged access improves the general orientation in the underground sections of the complex and generously sized passages and halls facilitate passenger flow. Each of the three levels—platform, retail floor, and aboveground station hall—serves a different function and is strictly separated from each other in spatial terms. This differentiation is also expressed in the materialization, creating readily identifiable locations.

Vertical means of access, such as stairs, escalators, and elevators are formed as continuous, solid-structure conveyance cores running through all the levels. Their geometry responds to the existing built surroundings, forming individual volumes that, in part, also perform structural functions, such as acting as bearings for existing supports in the heritage-listed roof of the railway station. The track positions in the new underground station could not be aligned to mirror those in the platform hall above and, therefore, necessitated the development of a special solution around the passenger elevators emerging from Löwenstrasse transit station. By using slanted shafts, the inclined elevator casings stand out spatially, acting as markers to the geometrical constraints of the infrastructure developments of the past decades.

The design of the subterranean spaces creates a distinct, friendly, and clear atmosphere. Light, smooth, and stylish surfaces transform the retail level into a modern center and circulation space and the same material and lighting concepts are applied in all of the halls and passages. The simple and robust material and color scheme in the open shop fronts, closed wall spaces, floors, and ceilings create a neutral spatial impression. The architecture is highly functional and dispenses with decoration, as the window displays, advertising, wayfinding, and people impart enough color. The architecture forms a calm backdrop to the signage, advertising, and uses of the station.

The underground platforms of Löwenstrasse transit station, together with the installation galleries illuminated by strip lighting, create islands of light. In contrast, the tunnel walls, railway tracks, and roofing over the tracks are kept dark. The warm color temperature of the strip lighting accentuates this centralized spatial impression.

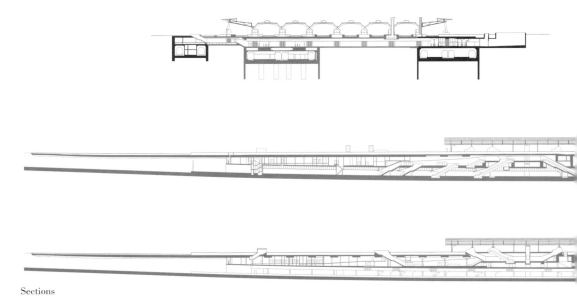

Sections

How do you resolve the unfavorable aspects of site conditions?

Site conditions are ever-present and build the base for every project. They are neither good nor bad. They enrich our ideas and position us toward the given task. First, abstract ideas are generated based on a profound analysis of the site's location and the place's history, as well as the programmatic, functional, and technical requirements. These are developed into design schemes that become the backup for every subsequent design step. The attitude toward the project is constantly adjusted and refined through the driving idea and conditions of the site.

How do you put forward solutions comprehensively and objectively without any prejudgments?

The analyses and the developed concepts allow an objective approach toward the project without prejudgments. Simultaneously, a personal ideology and position toward architecture is needed as a counter pole. This methodology is indispensable in tackling any task. Having an own position is the base to any design approach. Without one, you are lost.

How do you perceive the abstract architectural space?

I not only imagine myself moving in the space, I do it. It's movement that makes space perceivable and it is movement

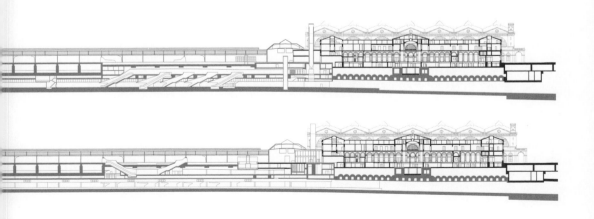

that's the origin, as well as the goal of every successful scheme. Additionally, movement makes space perceivable in time. In the Zürich main station, we imagined and built short, direct, clear, and neutral ways for the commuters. The passengers shouldn't be thinking about spatial obstacles but about their personal plans, hopes, and goals.

How do you coordinate the relationship between function, space, style, and circulation?

Functional, programmatic, formal, and structural ideas are tested based on the concept, and confronted constantly with the original analysis. With this method, diverse solutions are developed in infinite intermediate steps from the first sketch

to the final construction detail. This iterative process is very complex and prone to error, especially in long-term projects such as the Zürich station. During this process, the driving idea of the project can't be lost from sight at any time and each adjustment's compatibility with that idea has to be tested.

The inclined elevators are not a formal folie de grandeur, but a consequence of the position of the tracks in the new underground station, which couldn't be aligned to mirror those in the platform hall. The specific volumes of stairs and elevators in the hall act as bearings for the existing and protected roof of the railway station. All decisions respond to the function and to the existing built surroundings.

How do your plans and ideas contribute in deriving a design?

The design process is not linear. Phases and intermediate results build on each other, but there are always parallel ideas that can be brought in depending on the project's development. The amount of parallel ideas can be overwhelming, especially in the early stages, such as preliminary phases. A strong and clear position is crucial to staying radical.

How do you try to understand your clients' intentions?

Projects are developed further with large, multidisciplinary planning teams, the authorities, and the clients based on our concepts and designs. Endless effort needs to be made in order to preserve and improve the existing ideas without watering them down. Our task is to react to new requirements and to implement them in compliance with the project's principles. A flexible and strong basic concept is crucial for the collective development. Our partners understand our driving ideas; simultaneously, our design anticipates the changing parameters of our partners. A strong, consequent, and radical project can absorb changes and adjustments.

How do you incorporate your client's proposals into your design schemes?

New proposals and requirements need to be confronted with the basic concept: either they fit or they have to be made to fit. Sometimes they influence the concept, which leads to adjustments in already defined elements. For the project, these subsequent changes mean a lot of additional work in order not to lose its coherence and strength.

How do you make evaluations and judgments on your own schemes?

Our designs are very rational, functional, and are derived directly from their functions. They answer to present and timeless issues at the same time. We identify problems and solve them intelligently and precisely. This working method is comparable to that of an engineer. We are interested in structure, material, movement, program, and light, amongst many other things. Essentially, the origin of our designs is not architectural.

When designing, not all of an architect's ideas can always be fully realized. Could you share on how to handle such a situation?

Our experience from infinite competitions and built projects allows us to identify the potentials of our schemes very

early on and to conduct the design process effectively and
successfully. This also means that we know where we
have won or lost quality. The built project is never only the
built scheme. It is the sum of our discussions, changes,
improvements, and cutbacks, and therefore, has a life of its
own. Intellectually, the project belongs to us. In the case of
Zürich station, the built result belongs to society.

**When you worked on this project, how did you strive to maintain your
original idea from beginning to end?**

Discussion of solutions is a crucial part of the design
process. Sketches and drawings need intensive care and
examination on their way to built reality. We are not allowed
to stop reflecting, otherwise, we risk losing our ideas and
dreams. We need energy, patience, experience, and money
on the way to realization.

Site plan

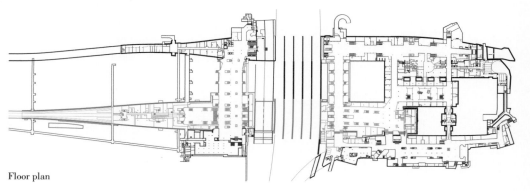

Floor plan

Analysis, concept, design, and realization evolve and correct themselves constantly without betraying the overall idea. Changes offer the opportunity to improve earlier decisions, some of which have to be given up in order to bring the project forward.

How do you make a comprehensive judgment on a design's progress and optimize the process?

The design process differs every time. It is dependent on infinite factors and a multitude of characters. A profound analysis in the beginning is essential in order not to lose one's way. The rest is intensive teamwork and a lot of persuasive efforts.

How do you identify critical problems and seek solutions?

Time and resources are the most critical factors. Each and every issue is solvable with time, patience, and money. Unfortunately,

it is exactly this which we lack. Crucial decisions have to be taken in minutes instead of days or months. Under this pressure, a lot of experience and caution is necessary in order to stay true to the main concept and to your personal principles.

What role does teamwork play in identifying problems that may have been overlooked?

Problems can't be avoided. They are an indicator of hidden issues, but they also reveal the different levels of involvement of the individual team members. In large teams, there are always varying interests and different limitations. The smallest common denominator is simply never good enough for any kind of solution. The motivation, social interaction, conveying of common goals, and enthusiasm for the project are the most important factors to successfully perform as a team. Patience and empathy with employees, colleagues, and clients lead to a productive working environment and subsequently, to a better project.

How do you respond to unexpected problems that occur during the design process?

Anything can happen—always, and in each and every area. The safer you feel, the more you think that everything is under control and the closer the next catastrophe is. Be ready.

"Always follow your intuition without prejudice."

Miguel de la Torre

Miguel de la Torre founded Miguel de la Torre Arquitectos, which develops residential and commercial projects of diverse scale and nature. The practice has grown with its clients over more than twenty-five years and collaborates with leading architecture and interior design firms. Special attention to details and a deep knowledge of the profession has allowed de la Torre's works to accomplish and exceed clients' expectations. The nature of materials and neutral color palettes balance and shape the spaces his practice creates.

PROJECT NAME---Liverpool Paseo Querétaro façade
LOCATION---Santiago de Querétaro, Mexico
COMPLETED---2017
AREA---95,799 square feet (8,900 square meters)
DESIGN---Miguel de la Torre Arquitectos
PHOTOGRAPHY---Jaime Navarro

Liverpool Paseo Querétaro is located at the Paseo Querétaro shopping center in Santiago de Querétaro, Mexico. The façade is a grid of hollowed-out triangular modules in white prefabricated concrete. Some of the hollows have a flat surface, while others have a subtracted pyramidical relief. The face of the triangles are orientated toward three different directions, thereby changing the angle of the pyramids within the grid. When combined, this creates visual texture, capturing the sun in an abstract play of light and shadows throughout the day.

How do you resolve the unfavorable aspects of site conditions?

The site is the first thing that must be analyzed before starting to design any project. Within these factors, we find data that cannot change, such as terrain conditions and restrictions—in our case, the volume and context of Paseo Querétaro shopping center.

Use these rules as an opportunity and not as a limitation to achieve an original architectural proposal and to exceed the expectations of the client. In this project, we needed to find an architectural façade that corresponded with the rectangular shape of the floor, and at the same time, with the interior program of the Liverpool warehouses.

How do you put forward solutions comprehensively and objectively without any prejudgments?

Always follow your intuition without prejudice. Never stay with the first solution that comes to your mind; try to solve the project in a simple way. Allow existing factors to be the ones that give you the correct answer. The best architectural proposals are always those that solve the problem in the most logical way.

Liverpool, being a department store, required the consideration of different factors for the development of its design. We had to solve elements, such as the material to be used, the colors, textures, and how they will all interact with the store logo in our design. We could have stayed safe with the "traditional" design line that the store is used to, but our instincts told us to look for something more—an aesthetic, functional, and innovative solution that responds to customer needs and our creative minds.

How do you perceive the abstract architectural space?

Before projecting, it is important to close your eyes and imagine yourself in the space. How does it feel to be inside and outside of it? What do you hear? How does it look? Define

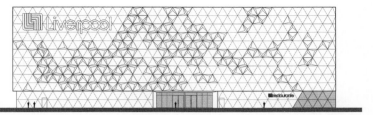

North elevation

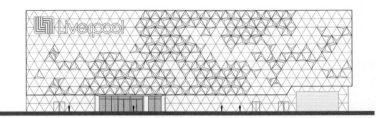

South elevation

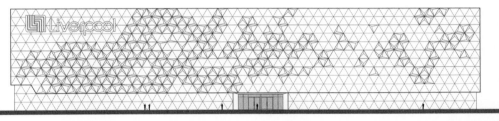

East elevation

the experience that you aim to transmit to all the users. Once you have that clear, you can start designing. Thus, within the infinity of options that exist, it will be easier to choose only one. On the Liverpool façade, the effect of the light and shadow invites you to take in the space at any time of the day—every moment in a different and unique way.

How do you coordinate the relationship between function, space, style, and circulation?

As an architectural project changes and matures, it is important that it always maintains consistency between all its factors. The project discourse must be clear and must develop in a linear way, being faithful to the original concept from beginning to end. For the façade, we considered the idea of designing a versatile module that could adapt to the interior and exterior needs of the warehouse by having windows and accesses without breaking with the triangular grid.

How do your plans and ideas contribute in deriving a design?

Design processes work like trial-and-error in architecture. Multiple options are analyzed before reaching the final result, and the importance of this process must not be forgotten. Save the different options you cover, remember all the steps you had to travel before reaching the final result, and use them to promote future projects. And always enjoy the process.

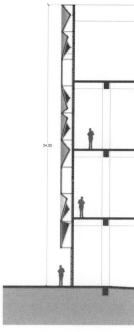

Section

Over time, you can have ideas in your head about a pattern, a texture, colors or spaces, but without a project as such. The Liverpool project was an opportunity to explore some of such types of ideas that did not have an exact form or enforcement.

How do you try to understand your clients' intentions?

Clear communication with the client is the key to a successful project. As architects, we must be empathetic toward the client and understand their needs in order to satisfy them. We are the translators of their wishes; through our creativity and knowledge, we must make them come true.

Right from the beginning of the Liverpool project, we tried to have clear and deep communication with the client about their needs and vision. The goal is to receive all the information that may contribute to the creative development of the project. This is how it's possible to capture and portray the essence and ideas of the client in a successful architectural work.

How do you incorporate your client's proposals into your design schemes?

The clients' proposals must be taken into account. We design each project to optimally fulfill its needs and provide solutions. As architects we must have the ability to mediate between the proposals or requests of the clients and our creative works. It is not always possible to express exactly what our clients ask for, but it is possible to find solutions to their concerns, so we meet their needs while remaining harmonious with the project.

How do you make evaluations and judgments on your own schemes?

The key to success is to never stop wondering and settling for anything. Living each experience in a unique and unrepeatable way is what allows us to improve our architecture. Knowing your project and always keeping

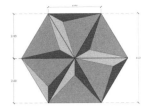

Module

in mind what the final goal is helps us to make assertive decisions throughout the process. Knowing which are the moments that need more attention and which are the ones that you can be more flexible in facilitates planning and developing and, therefore, the evaluation of the project from start to the end.

How do you stay curious in complex and disordered situations?

By finding several ways of seeing things. Distinct approaches to attacking problems and asking for different opinions will open the panorama to design different, increasingly original things. Stay sensitive to your surroundings. Look for inspiration in your own life—music, food, travel, books, feelings, relationships, and so on.

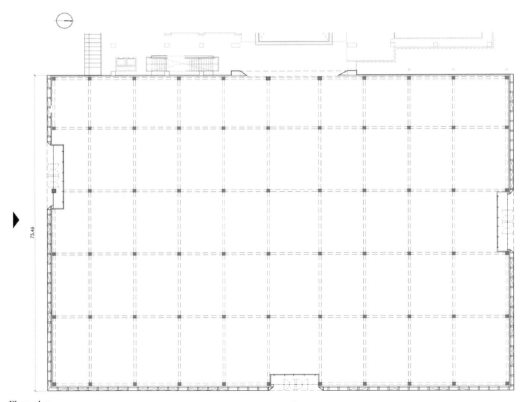

Floor plan

When designing, not all of an architect's ideas can always be fully realized. Could you share on how to handle such a situation?

Avoid discarding ideas definitely. Sometimes, it is good to leave a project aside and return to it later. This changes the focus of it and gives you a new opportunity to create even more innovative projects.

When you worked on this project, how did you strive to maintain your original idea from beginning to end?

Sometimes, we can lose direction in the design process, given the infinity of options that exist. It is important to stay certain and to realize that you are starting to lose the original idea of the project. If so, it is time to pause, look back, and remember the concepts that will lead you to obtain what you are looking for.

In a design process, it is normal to explore different ideas to arrive at a final concept. The important thing is to know how to explore and land them in such a way that they don't become endless. During the design of Liverpool's façade, it was necessary to be clear about the moments of creativity and exploration of concepts, as well as the moments of definitions and development of the chosen concept.

How do you make a comprehensive judgment on a design's progress and optimize the process?

Having a clear judgment regarding your work is basic, avoiding at all times to let these judgments stop the inertia that propels the project. We must see the limitations of time as an opportunity to exploit creativity. Endless projects can be exhausting. Optimizing the process helps make it easier to work on them and achieve a better result.

Judgments about our process does not necessarily have a negative connotation. Knowing them gives us the opportunity

to use them as an advantage; it helps us to manage the time, ideas, and the different moments of the process. It helps us to know and explore more of our resources, opportunities, weaknesses, and therefore, the project as a whole.

How do you identify critical problems and seek solutions?

There will come a time when you think you have found the solution and this solution sometimes brings with it a different problem. Do not despair. Breathe and take a moment to rest your mind. Every process must be enjoyed, including the search for several solutions. When we begin to develop any project, we try to see all the possible scenarios along with the complications that could exist in each one; this helps us to go one step forward, avoiding or managing complications. While developing the Liverpool project, knowing the project deeply helped us to solve problems in a more efficient and agile way. The secret is to enjoy it and see that each of these "problems" are one more step toward a great project and a lesson learned for the future.

What role does teamwork play in identifying problems that may have been overlooked?

Teamwork is a great way to create incredible projects. As they say, two heads are better than one. In this case, the more eyes you have to see with, the better. There are different points of view and new approaches that emerge in a team. Take it as an opportunity to find problems that have not been taken into account before and come to a solution as a whole.

How do you respond to unexpected problems that occur during the design process?

Having unexpected situations is a great way to exploit creativity. Thinking about all kinds of possible scenarios forces the mind to open up. Resort to anything, even if it seems unreasonable. You can be surprised.

"It is important to have multiple discussions with clients and understand the intentions of all involved."

Storaket Architectural Studio

Storaket Architectural Studio is an all-inclusive architecture practice that creates innovative and cutting-edge designs, combining aesthetics and functionality. The studio offers urban planning, architecture, engineering, construction management, and interior design services, and has been involved in architectural projects in Armenia and Moscow. This includes schools, private homes, apartments, multi-use buildings, banks, and workplaces. Storaket actively participates in national and international competitions, bringing fresh and creative ideas, and a strong experience in managing construction.

PROJECT NAME---C building, Ayb School
LOCATION---Yerevan, Armenia
COMPLETED---2017
AREA---45,208 square feet (4,200 square meters)
DESIGN---Storaket Architectural Studio
PHOTOGRAPHY---Sona Manukyan, Ani Avagyan

The C building was designed for Ayb School and it's slated for use as the elementary school and, in the future, as the middle school. The building is situated in front of the A and B buildings and can accommodate 240 students. Just as in A and B, the architectural philosophy of C lies in creating an open and collaborative educational environment that is multifunctional and which allows for learning to take place in multiple ways.

The building's first floor integrates an open space with an amphitheater and also leads to the workshops in the basement. The interior of

the first floor is connected to the exterior landscape through hidden openings and walkways, allowing easy access to the outside by giving students the opportunity to leave the building and commune with nature. A large white block sits on the deep-colored base level of the building and houses the second and third floors.

The exteriors of A, B, and C are substantially different, while the internal organization is the same. Everything relating to the educational process, such as classrooms, is situated on the upper floors, and social areas, such as the hall and cafeteria, are positioned on the lower floor. The C building is equipped with modern educational technologies, laboratories, art and crafts studios, a sports hall, an amphitheater, game and recreation zones, and a library. The concrete walls are largely exposed and have been treated with a water-repellent coating. All wiring and communication engineering is exposed and a low-key color scheme is used throughout the building. There is no plasterboard and paint is kept to a minimum.

The rooms have access to natural light despite the basement being submerged 13 feet (4 meters) below ground. The boundaries of the excavation go far beyond the contours of the building, forming a free perimeter for walking and going out into the yard. This also creates a green roof on a portion of the building.

The building was developed with energy efficiency in mind and includes an energy-efficient air-conditioning system. Solar panels are mounted on the southern façade and a proprietary technology developed by the design team uses sensors to automatically position the solar panels where the sun's rays are most abundant. Also developed and implemented is a special self-powered (photosensitive) system that automatically tints windows in the event of excess light.

How do you resolve the unfavorable aspects of site conditions?

Before starting any project, our studio performs a comprehensive site analysis to disclose any challenges and outline any advantages of the natural conditions. Difficult site conditions normally provide the main idea to tailor the flow and circulation of the structure. For the Ayb C building, we were obligated to have a lower ground floor (-1 level) based on site and soil analysis. Therefore, we utilized it for activity-related spaces and other multipurpose rooms.

How do you put forward solutions comprehensively and objectively without any prejudgments?

It is impossible for two designs to look the same. It is in our nature to challenge ourselves with every new project.

Western elevation

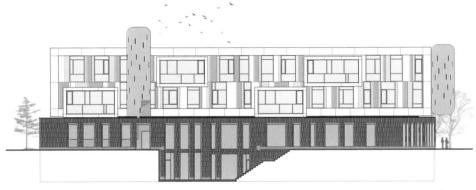

Northern elevation

We use our experience, inspirations, and ideas to brainstorm a concept and design everything from scratch. For Ayb C, the initial concept was changed multiple times as it was imperative that the project kicked-off with the right design. Lots of ideas changed based on the zonings, functions of the spaces, and the changing requirements of the client. The approaches of the participants are different and the best solution always comes after several discussions and a clear review of the project.

How do you perceive the abstract architectural space?

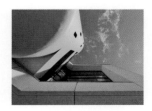

It is very important, especially for an educational building, that the flow of the spaces harmonize well with the needs of the students. In particular, the choreography of the building can highlight positive aspects and hide negative ones. The Ayb C building is an open and collaborative educational space that allows students to easily access the outside for communing with nature. The building has classrooms on

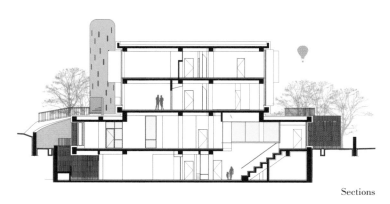

Sections

the upper floors and a cafeteria and workshop spaces on the lower floors, maintaining a flow similar to the other buildings on campus. This consistency was important and had to be maintained.

How do you coordinate the relationship between function, space, style, and circulation?

In the Ayb C building, we created specific zones within the circulation of the building that have separate functions. The layout of each zone was driven by functionality. The relationship between function, space, and design comes from the notion that space is multifunctional. Once we confirmed this idea, the design was led by the overarching concept of multifunctionality. The space of the C building is open and not separated. Therefore, it creates an ideal design for an educational facility with a contemporary environment.

How do your plans and ideas contribute in deriving a design?

The idea of how today's students understand their educational environment and how that environment shapes their expectations was at the core of our design. Uncertainty of the future and the intensity of new challenges train them to be more flexible and more adaptable to their environment. In an open space such as the C building, students learn to find new opportunities by using the school space in a more creative way.

With more than eleven years of experience, we think that the best ideas are usually some of the initial ones, and even if they aren't applicable for a specific project, recording them is a must. Different solutions can come in handy for different situations and projects.

How do you try to understand your clients' intentions?

The schematic solutions could change from the beginning of the project after reviewing it with the parties involved. Obviously, it is important to predetermine the expectations, requirements, and needs of the client. We prioritize doing this before getting our hands dirty and diving in headfirst. It is important to have multiple discussions with the clients and understand the intentions of all involved. After presenting what we believe is the correct solution based on our analysis of the site and other requirements, we make sure that all parties involved are on the same page before moving forward.

How do you incorporate your client's proposals into your design schemes?

It is very important to work as a team with everyone involved in the project. Comprehensive communication is key to a seamless work process. For example, the initial design of Ayb C included stone for the façade. However, after careful consideration of seismic standards and the fact that Ayb C would serve as a school building, we communicated the need to review the material to be used on the façade. We discussed the issue and decided on a lighter solution such as plaster. This was a result of proactive communication, which created a win-win situation for all parties. It is important to always keep the client in the loop and ask for feedback. Incorporating ideas along the way is a part of the design process. Some are good, some are bad, and it boils down to simple communication and an objective analysis on whether a specific idea will work or not.

How do you make evaluations and judgments on your own schemes?

The plans for Ayb C were different in the beginning compared to the end result, but with all the decision-making we had to do during the process, we stayed true to the initial concept. What made it difficult was that instead of having just the client (the owners), we had many other parties we had to communicate with, including the general contractors, engineers, and other specialists. It is very important to listen to specialists and the other participants' ideas, and also find a way to realize your solutions at the same time through perseverance.

How do you stay curious in complex and disordered situations?

To enjoy the creation process is the most important part of the project. This is why we take on any challenge with curiosity and the motivation to find a solution. For the Ayb C building, we discussed our design in the schematic stage with engineers and general contractors to obtain and understand their working solutions to minimize challenges down the road.

When designing, not all of an architect's ideas can always be fully realized. Could you share on how to handle such a situation?

Effective design will curate solutions that can be implemented in projects later on. It is very important to know what the initial design was and to record the first concepts despite not executing them.

When you worked on this project, how did you strive to maintain your original idea from beginning to end?

This is the hardest part of every single project. Reality and the concept clash all the time; this is not an exact and formulated process because it is difficult to put boundaries on creativity. So, we abide by this core workflow: we trust our creativity at the beginning, our management and problem-solving skills through the process, and our professionalism at the end when we deliver the project to our happy clients.

How do you make a comprehensive judgment on a design's progress and optimize the process?

Making a comprehensive judgment on the design progress is good for two reasons. First, it identifies any shortfalls that need to be reconsidered, redone, or rethought. Second, it identifies solutions that may not be for the specific project but could be very helpful in a different project. It is, therefore, sometimes important to have someone else from the team, who is not completely involved in that specific project, to pitch in and help with fresh ideas and constructive criticism. That is why a team is really important for architects. Sometimes, it gives a chance to double-check the solutions.

After building the previous two buildings of Ayb School and also the FabLab Building on-site, we had lots of

insight as to what the client needs and, therefore, we were more prepared when it came to the C building project. This allowed us to have an even more optimized process, allowing the project to be carried out smoothly.

How do you identify critical problems and seek solutions?

At the end of the day, all parties involved, including us as architects and designers, want to see a fully functioning building that properly serves its purpose. To do that, we need to tackle every single problem and find a solution no matter the cost. The initial design of the building has great value. However, it is easy to design a building without building it. What defines true design is going through the process of compromising and being creative to execute your design without losing its main objective. There can be problems that require major changes, but it will succeed as long as all parties involved are happy with the outcome and the building serves its design concept.

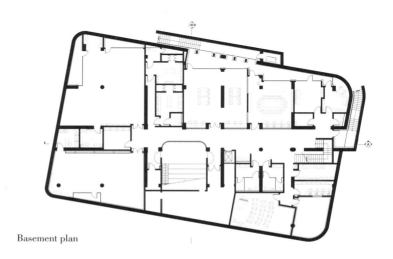

Basement plan

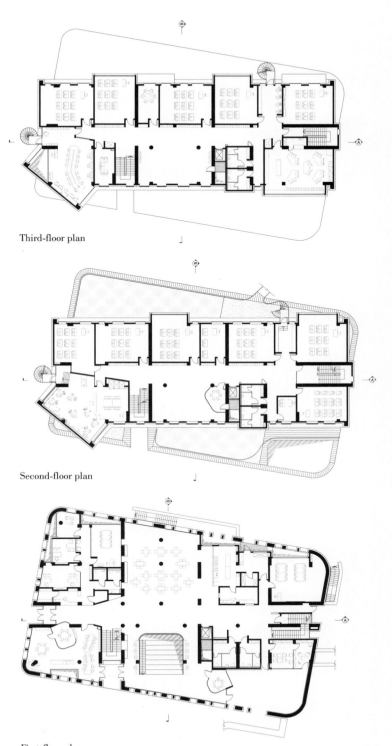

Third-floor plan

Second-floor plan

First-floor plan

What role does teamwork play in identifying problems that may have been overlooked?

> Teamwork is essential to finding problems that may have been overlooked. For Ayb C, teamwork didn't just mean working within our studio. Teamwork meant collaborating with all parties involved to review and audit each other in a professional and consistent manner to identify anything that may have been overlooked. Reviewing the project with colleagues, engineers, and specialists is very important, and to have critical judgment that leads to a final solution is the best way to move forward.

How do you respond to unexpected problems that occur during the design process?

> We always like to refrain from panicking. When encountering an unexpected big issue, we take a breath and let the philosophy, concept, and core design of the project speak for themselves. If all the things mentioned were kept consistent during the design process, then a solution will most probably present itself. In other words, the core idea of the project and the logic behind it will lead you to the best answers for unexpected problems.

"Do not cross out even the bravest ideas."

JM Studio Architek- toniczne

Magdalena Ignaczak and Jacek Kunca founded JM Studio Architektoniczne in 1992. JM Studio designs architecture, interiors, and landscapes, and Ignaczak and Kunca believe that the architectural concept of a building or interior is only the beginning. Precise finishing is equally important. Therefore, the team undertakes and supervises all of its projects down to the smallest detail. JM Studio also tries to implement its projects as a general contractor or substitute investor.

PROJECT NAME---Intop Office
LOCATION---Warsaw, Poland
COMPLETED---2017
AREA---10,549 square feet
(980 square meters)
DESIGN---JM Studio
Architektoniczne
Magdalena Ignaczak, Jacek Kunca
PHOTOGRAPHY---Mariusz Purta

The office is the headquarters of Intop, a civil engineering firm. The building consists of three overlapping cuboids with different heights and materials. The façade materials—Corten steel, concrete, steel, and gabions—tie back the architectural theme to civil engineering, being civil engineering materials. They don't require maintenance and will build up patina with age. Large glass surfaces make the building look lighter, as well as connect the architecture with the internal space, so that the view of the interior becomes part of the exterior, and the view of the outside world becomes part of the interior.

The building appears to have two fronts due to the plot size, location and land-use plan. A more formal front is viewed from the direction of the main street, which meets the gabion façade, while the actual entrance is through the small backyard. The building is visible from all sides and each façade is, therefore, different and distinctive. The northern façade has two large glass bay windows and an industrial-style external metal staircase. The southern façade has a longitudinal window with Corten crosses to diffuse sunlight and obstruct the view of a neighboring building. The west façade is a 32.8-feet-tall (10-meter-tall) monumental wall of gabions filled with granite aggregate that looks attractive in daylight, as well as at night when illuminated. The eastern façade is the most tranquil and distinguished, housing the entrance, which is accessed via a steel bridge.

Each floor has a different function and a different design, although they speak the same architectural language: ribbed concrete ceilings, concrete floors and walls, and glass walls and doors. Almost all furniture and details are designed individually and constitute an integral part of the interior.

The large external and internal glass surfaces bring ample daylight inside; artificial lighting is needed only after working hours. Overlapping space creates a feeling of togetherness and facilitates communication, while ensuring the quietness necessary for work. All technical systems are hidden, enabling the concrete structure to be exposed inside the building.

How do you resolve the unfavorable aspects of site conditions?

Sometimes, the more limitations, the more interesting the final effect. Limitations stimulate, increase creativeness, and force us to think how we can transform shortcomings into advantages. The limitations in the Intop project— local regulations, an unattractive neighborhood, a noisy road, and the client's expectations of a representative headquarters—contributed to a very individual, place-specific effect.

How do you put forward solutions comprehensively and objectively without any prejudgments?

You must have a clear head all the time; be open to different changes and not be stuck to one concept. First comes a functional analysis taking into account external limitations. Then, in the result of hard work and next approximations, a building's solid crystallizes. For Intop, we had to include additional distant perspectives from which the building would be visible. A unique starting point was the idea to use Corten steel, gabions, and concrete both outside and inside.

How do you perceive the abstract architectural space?

A design process requires time, but first, it is important to determine how users will function in the created space; how the building will be perceived by employees and guests; what emotions the space will evoke; how it will influence the company image; and what customers will think before entering the CEO's office, and so on.

How do you coordinate the relationship between function, space, style, and circulation?

The architectural design of Intop Office was created simultaneously with the interior design and together, they form an inseparable whole and interact with each other. Thanks to that, the interior becomes a part of the architecture and the façades become a part of the interior. At a certain stage, even the architectural design was stopped in order to fine-tune the interior design.

How do your plans and ideas contribute in deriving a design?

At each stage of the design and construction of Intop Office, we had control over the whole. The building was designed by us in its entirety from the concept, working model, architectural design, and interior design, to the finest details.

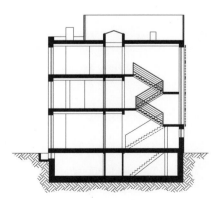
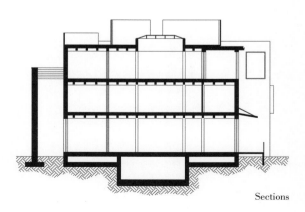

Sections

How do you try to understand your clients' intentions?

Understanding the real intentions of our clients is always a challenge. The client's expectations are often contradictory. Sometimes, a client cannot express clearly their expectations and we have to rely on our intuition. An architect's role is to creatively process the client's expectations.

How do you incorporate your client's proposals into your design schemes?

The cooperation between an architect and a client in the design process is necessary. Good listening skills are also

important. An architect is a guide, but it is not them who is the most important. It is not an architect who will use a designed building. It is essential to write down the client's guidelines and expectations, which are always the basis for designing. Our target is to design and build the best possible building.

How do you make evaluations and judgments on your own schemes?

We have to set a high bar, not be afraid of brave ideas, and persistently look for technical solutions for them according to the principle that we are limited only by our own imagination and our client's budget. The best design is always the next one.

How do you stay curious in complex and disordered situations?

You have to look for your own way. The more difficult, the better. On one hand, you have to avoid being trapped in making the work easier with trivial solutions. On the other hand, you also have to avoid unnecessary flamboyance and fashionable trends that will shortly become outdated.

When designing, not all of an architect's ideas can always be fully realized. Could you share on how to handle such a situation?

Do not cross out even the bravest ideas. Sooner or later, there will be favorable circumstances to make them come true— such as a more open and conscious investor or a larger budget. You certainly should not be discouraged. An architect's traits should be perseverance, patience, and consistency.

When you worked on this project, how did you strive to maintain your original idea from beginning to end?

Sometimes, by focusing too strong and too long on solving one design problem, you can lose the needed perspective. It is good to have a break then and take some distance. It goes a long way at times to step back a little. Sometimes, it is also good to work on two projects that are in different design stages at the same time. Unfortunately, there are regulations in Poland and an architect loses control over his work after receiving a building permit; plus, designing architecture together with the interior is rare. Very often, the interior is designed separately by another who may have no place in architecture. With the Intop Office project, thanks to our hard struggle, we managed to have control and influence on the realization of both. And thanks to this, the building is 100 percent compatible with the design.

How do you make a comprehensive judgment on a design's progress and optimize the process?

Although an architect is, in a way, a visionary and likes to build castles in the air, they must also be down-to-earth and keep deadlines, and ensure compliance with regulations, the targeted program, and the clients' expectations. It is all about balancing and looking for a perfect balance. The design of Intop Office was not easy. We were under pressure all the time because the investor did not understand that a well-thought-out design with many individual solutions requires more time. This generated many conflicts and difficulties. As we participated in the realization of this

First-floor plan   Second-floor plan   Third-floor plan

building, many elements were also designed and corrected during construction and furnishing.

How do you identify critical problems and seek solutions?

You have to be fully concentrated all the time. You must not fall into routine, but control everything almost obsessively. Sometimes a final design is very different from the original concept. It is necessary then to check that changes did not go too far. The final decision depends on the investor.

What role does teamwork play in identifying problems that may have been overlooked?

Theoretically, teamwork should make project control and management easier. In practice, a main designer is responsible for taking complex care of the project and the details. Almost every associate who is engaged in some part of the project instinctively wants to take a shortcut because they look only at their job.

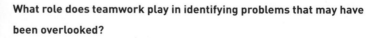

In the Intop Office project, only our control, constant supervision of the whole, and treating different parts of the project comprehensively and not as detached fragments gave the intended effect.

How do you respond to unexpected problems that occur during the design process?

An architect must control the entire project, balance contradictory interests, and sometimes fight for their rights in order not to lose control over the project. It is not easy, but it is a necessity in order to satisfy both the client and architect.

The architect must be almost like Leonardo da Vinci and have interdisciplinary theoretical and practical knowledge—by being artist, engineer, craftsman, psychologist, negotiator, and estimator, and in each of these distant areas, they must be able to move efficiently and develop themselves all the time.

"Like a cook, it seems important to be able to let the dough rest and to take the necessary distance before continuing."

Jean-Pascal Crouzet

Jean-Pascal Crouzet completed his studies at the National School of Architecture of Grenoble in 1989. He joined Studios Architecture International in Paris in 1992 and spent six months in the agency's main office in San Francisco. Crouzet directed several major projects in Paris and across Europe for large companies based in Silicon Valley. In 1997, he joined the London office to develop Phase 2 of the research and development campus at 3Com in Hemel Hempstead. On returning to Paris, Crouzet became associate architect. He left Studios Architecture in early 2000 to establish Lautrefabrique Architects with his architect wife, Nadia Crouzet.

PROJECT NAME---Gymnase Carrier
LOCATION---Saint-Marcellin, France
COMPLETED---2013
AREA---23,681 square feet (2,200 square meters)
DESIGN---Lautrefabrique Architects
PHOTOGRAPHY---Luc Boegly

Gymnase Carrier is part of the Ecolé du Stade school campus. Architect H. Pelissier designed the gymnasium in the mid-1960s, along with the collection of buildings that make up the campus and it has been used continuously since its construction.

In 2011, the Municipality of Saint-Marcellin engaged Lautrefabrique to help revitalize the Ecolé du Stade campus. The design team determined that the architectural integrity of Gymnase Carrier was worthy of preservation and focused efforts toward restoration and renovation.

Lautrefabrique designed and installed signage to help visitors and passersby identify the use of the structure. This includes a signage on the roof that can be seen from the road, three large sports silhouettes on the wall of the adjoining building (to represent its purpose), and a totem pole made with stones that had originally been used in the gate posts of the gymnasium. Color accents were added to enliven the building, while the façade, apertures, and roofing were reconditioned such that they give people the perception that very little has been changed. The existing canopy entrance was preserved and the glass doors inside the entryway replaced with a window identical to the original. Color is also added to the main façade with colored LED lights in the canopies and mast. These lights activate at dusk and allow for identification of the building at night.

Inside the gym, a large sloping wood-clad wall adds a sense of warmth and separates the main gymnasium space from the locker and restroom areas. The overlapping wood used in the wall construction galvanizes the entire space and improves the acoustic qualities of the space. Polycarbonate panels on the south wall of the gym were replaced with more energy-efficient versions and the emergency exits were outfitted with steel-framed doors. Wood cladding is also installed in the hallway leading to lockers and restrooms; their entry and exits have been relocated to improve pedestrian flow. A new weightlifting area is created by way of a second-story glassed-in area that overlooks the main gymnasium, providing visual connection from above and below.

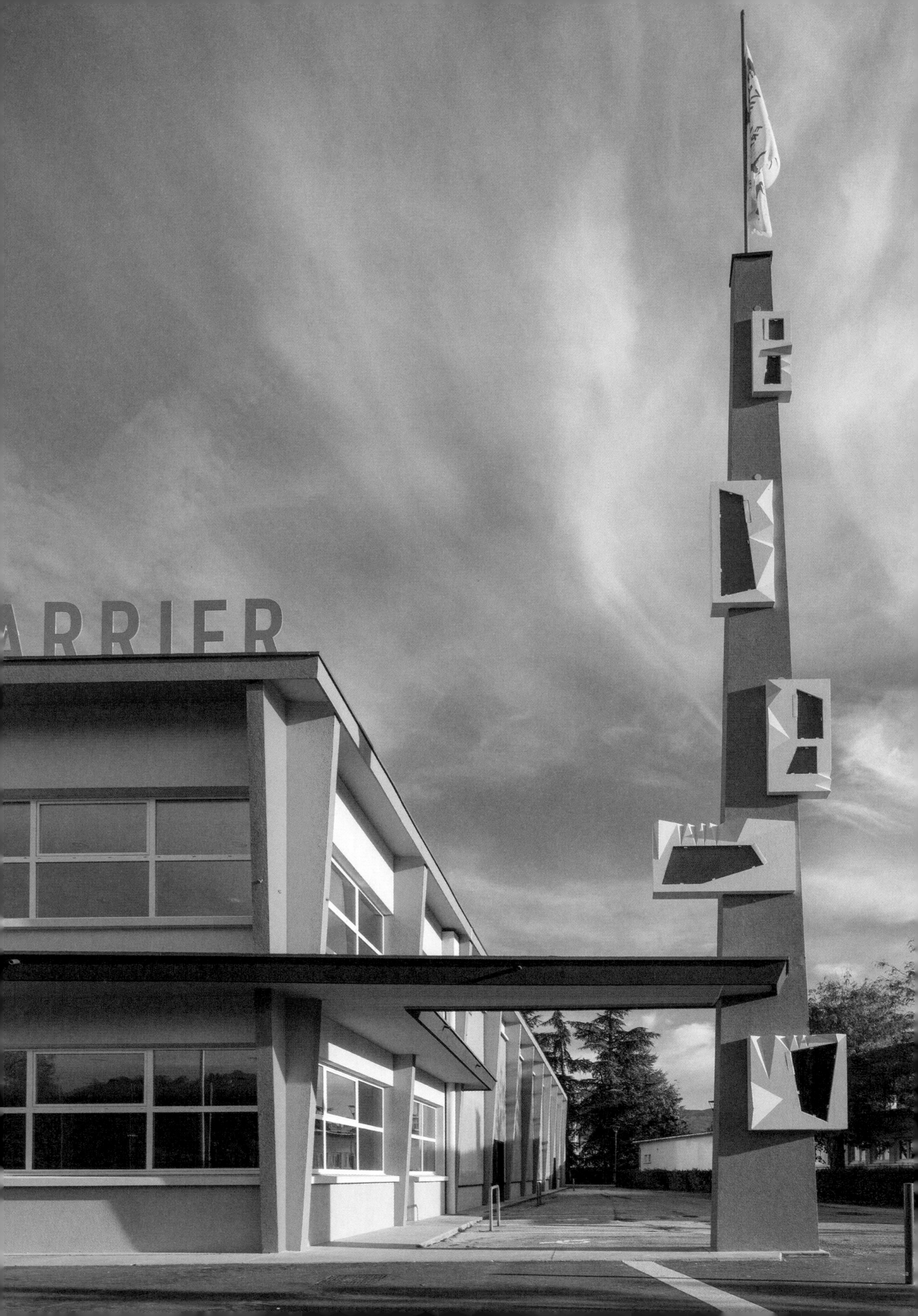
ARRIER

How do you resolve the unfavorable aspects of site conditions?

In the renovation of Gymnase Carrier, a detailed analysis of the elements to be preserved, valued, and revitalized allowed us to avoid the traps of a program that proposed thermal insulation from the outside. By augmenting the program to preserve the original moldings of the building, we were able to determine that the rear gable, which did not present any particular architectural character, could be covered with thermal insulation on the outside. This was one way to solve an unfavorable factor.

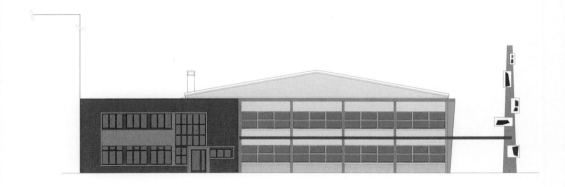

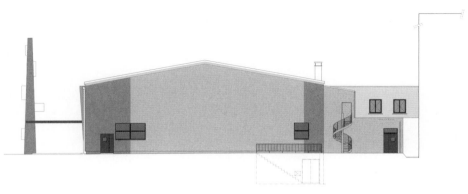

Elevations

How do you put forward solutions comprehensively and objectively without any prejudgments?

It is impossible to approach a project without any prejudgments. Whatever the project, each of us has an a priori view of the subject raised and of the subject to be treated. So, if we talk about a swimming pool without defining it further, for example, everyone will have their own idea of the swimming pool. Some will imagine it in the shape of a Californian peanut while others see it as a long swimming pool channel, or even as an ecological natural pool. It, therefore, is very important to us to be able to identify, from the start of the project, the prejudgments and

the a priori images of each participant and each member of the design team.

How do you perceive the abstract architectural space?

It is indeed essential to project into a space to check, as much as possible, how users will understand the different volumes. Thanks to modeling tools, we can now perform simulations to avoid errors and unnecessary expenses.

For the Carrier gymnasium, the client was keen to install bleachers on the mezzanine. 3D modeling allowed us to demonstrate that the spectators sitting on the stands would only have partial view of the playing area because of the width

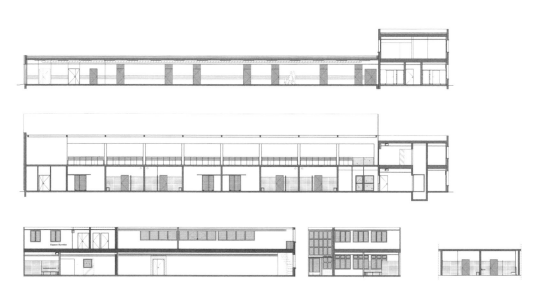

Cross sections

of the pillars that form the blinkers. In the end, we were able to leave the mezzanine space free of any steps and offer a wide handrail that can comfortably support spectators as they follow the game with an unobstructed view of the entire playing field. Moreover, the space without the mezzanine allows other sports practices for school children.

How do you coordinate the relationship between function, space, style, and circulation?

As part of a rehabilitation, such as that of Gymnase Carrier, the relationships between functions and pre-existing spaces were examined and questioned in light of new practices. Circulations and accesses to the changing rooms and toilets, and to the training area had to be changed. The changing rooms are now directly connected to the rear traffic connecting the entrance hall "dirty feet" and the training area "clean feet."

How do your plans and ideas contribute in deriving a design?

An alert mechanism is switched on as soon as a project starts, so any event or element can generate an idea related to the problem of the project. These ideas should be recorded in the most favorable form, be it sketch photo, note, and so on. These elements form a database, which we can draw from during the development of the project.

How do you try to understand your clients' intentions?

We strongly encourage the contribution and involvement of project owners and users throughout the duration of the project. Establishing a detailed program makes it possible to very clearly define the client's intentions. In addition, a series of interviews with the various and future users of Gymnase Carrier ensured that no user, nor uses, are left out.

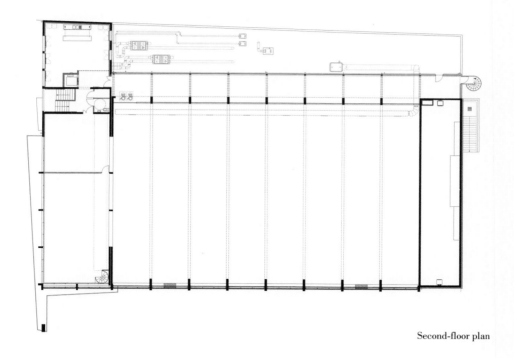

Second-floor plan

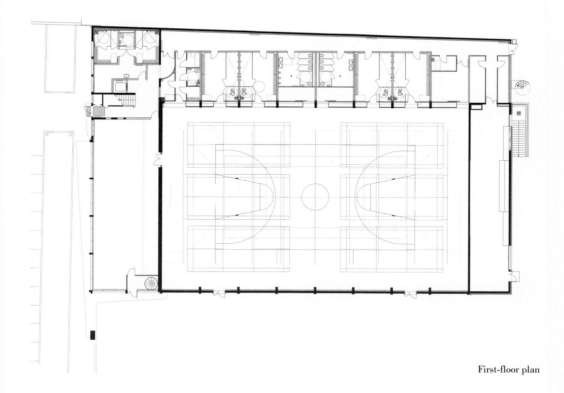

First-floor plan

How do you incorporate your client's proposals into your design schemes?

At the first instance, the client is at the heart of the development of the basic concept and the definition of functional needs. Past that, their guidelines are enriched and supported by the continuous contribution of the entire team in the development of the project. Our structured and participative work methodology allows us to involve both end users and consultants during the programming and design phases.

How do you make evaluations and judgments on your own schemes?

In the case of the Carrier gymnasium, it was necessary to show humility and respect toward the architect whose work was being rehabilitated. The confrontation within the agency between the different schemes proposed by the team allows us to select the one that suits the greatest number.

How do you stay curious in complex and disordered situations?

Complex and haphazard situations can be creative when you are able to overcome them. Curiosity is certainly not the first quality needed to deal with this type of situation, but it probably allows us to understand the facts that have led to complexity and disorder.

When designing, not all of an architect's ideas can always be fully realized. Could you share on how to handle such a situation?

The new design tools of assistance, which are becoming more powerful every day, allow the architect to transcend their most complex ideas. The production of data files from the architect's software allows companies to create the imagined volumes. It seems that there is no more limit today than that of cost. As a result, some ideas which cannot be realized temporarily may be realized in the future.

When you worked on this project, how did you strive to maintain your original idea from beginning to end?

Like a cook, it seems important to be able to let the dough rest and to take the necessary distance before continuing. Do not back down, but be able to realize when the project is deriving from the original scheme, while identifying the potentialities that can nest in any drift.

How do you make a comprehensive judgment on a design's progress and optimize the process?

The process of creating and developing a project is idiosyncratic. While there are procedures for driving the development of a project, there is nothing to determine the speed at which good ideas will emerge. From the start of the creative process, a schedule is established and it marks out the different stages of the project and phases for the delivery of documents to the client, who also has a set time to formulate his or her responses and comments.

How do you identify critical problems and seek solutions?

Problem identification does not always arise from the start
of the project, and some may even have been missed by the
client's program. Identifying problems is a secure guarantee
to improve the project development process. Our client on
the Gymnase Carrier project was insistent about wanting
bleachers installed above the changing rooms, but given the
existing structure of the training area, this would have, in a
way, created blinders and the spectators' view-span would
have been cut off by the existing concrete columns—this
would have allowed only a very partial view of the playground.
A computer simulation convinced the client and they agreed
to give up the bleachers for an area bordered by a guardrail,

and which has a large handrail that spectators can lean on and follow the matches.

What role does teamwork play in identifying problems that may have been overlooked?

Convinced that the confrontation of visions and different experiences is beneficial to the projects, we associate the skills and sensitivity of engineers, designers, landscapers, and lighting designers with our skills and sensitivity. The use of the latest computer technologies allows us to communicate with our customers and partners and produce the needed elements and results through all phases of the project. This pooling of skills favors the objective definition of the solution best suited to the needs of our customers and enables adequate response to the specificities of their project.

How do you respond to unexpected problems that occur during the design process?

Unforeseen problems usually arise during the construction phase if the design has been incorrectly completed. As part of countering this, the presence of the architect on-site is essential because the unexpected can also give rise to beautiful surprises and to opportunities to enrich the original design, or correct the shot.

"Drawing is the language of architecture and the tool that conveys ideas and thought."

Che Fu Chang

Founded by Steven Che Fu Chang, Che Fu Chang Architects is a mid-sized architecture firm based in Taipei. Chang graduated from the Pratt Institute in New York with a master's degree and specializing in tropical architecture. He then worked at Edward Larrabee Barnes Associates in New York and established his own practice in 1978, and has since designed diverse projects ranging from residential compounds to museums, MRT stations, and warehouses. Over the recent years, the firm has been focusing on comprehensive building typologies, mixing playful and practical ideas into smart architectural solutions.

PROJECT NAME---Alps Logistics Republic, Taichung
LOCATION---Taichung, Taiwan, China
COMPLETED---2017
AREA---398,867 square feet (37,056 square meters)
DESIGN---Che Fu Chang Architects
PHOTOGRAPHY---Studio Millspace

Located within a developing area close to the high-speed railway station, Alps Logistics Republic, Taichung is a warehouse for circulating goods and parcels. The design team wanted to create a hub not only for goods, but also for people as it is located near the station and can be seen by people standing on the station platform. Start-up offices and small-sized retail outlets were added to the program, transforming it into a hybrid, rather than simply being a mono-functional warehouse. These new elements also enabled the design team to transform the typical warehouse design stereotype, which was a massive box with little public interface.

A 65.6-foot (20-meter) setback on the east side and a double-story arcade evokes a highly interactive commercial street. Double rows of large trees, stairs interlocked with decks, and diverse street furniture are arranged along the street to encourage movement. The general public can access a sky garden via the steel staircase on the east façade. Linear windows provide a glimpse into the warehouse and the staircase landings provide spaces for rest and interaction. Lush climbing plants will gradually cover the staircase and become a green artery from the ground to the sky garden.

How do you resolve the unfavorable aspects of site conditions?

The site of Alps Logistics Republic is situated within a redevelopment close to the high-speed train station in Taiwan's second largest city, Taichung. The project was the first in the area since it was established in 2007. There were no clues of context nor adjacency, so we had to be careful about how the development would carry on once the building was complete.

Since the building is a warehouse, it would have to function mainly as a machine circulating goods and parcels. Hence, the lack of public interaction was predictable. Therefore, the discussion of "what more can we propose?" was raised. Since the site is so close to the high-speed railway station and people standing on the platform can easily spot it, we deliberated whether it would be possible to create a structure that would be prominent and engaging enough to draw in people in order to catalyze its "street vibrancy." Ultimately, it boiled down to this: could we make a public space to balance the industrial-oriented site? That specific motivation helped us to identify the key theme, which became the driving force of the design.

How do you put forward solutions comprehensively and objectively without any prejudgments?

We designed the warehouse in different perspectives, hoping to deconstruct the industry's typical design logic, which is to maximize return on investment. Instead of kicking off the design with a calculator, the project started with seeking opportunities to support and make way for the presence of people in an industrial workplace. The potential circulation was carefully mapped and demonstrated to speculate its accesses and routes. A series of public spaces, which are normally ignored in a warehouse design, were integrated to stimulate interactions.

We believe that an inspirational, highly interactive workplace will enhance the internal cohesion between workers and enterprise. The strategy of creating a hub, not only for goods but also for people, was, therefore, carried out. To take advantage of the site's proximity to a major public transportation center, we added start-up offices and retail outlets to the program as a game changer.

How do you perceive the abstract architectural space?

It is important to review the design through a pedestrian's point of view to help control the scale and atmosphere of the spaces inside and outside. Everything that might affect people's experience, including textures, materials, colors, sunlight, winds, accessibility, and so on, should be carefully considered to ensure the design quality when it is completed.

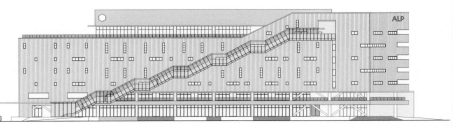

East elevation

That is why we faced the roof garden toward the east at Alps Logistics Republic. You can not only get a great view of the high-speed trains bustling by, but can also enjoy a comfortable shaded area on a sunny afternoon, which is significant in subtropical cities. The large staircase is almost like the public "spokesperson" that bridges the roof garden and the street. It had to be a delightful journey to encourage people to climb up and explore. That is why we carefully adjusted the dimension of the steps and arranged platforms outside each floor, hoping to create a playful social space, not just an eye-catching accessory that ferries people up and down.

How do you coordinate the relationship between function, space, style, and circulation?

With so many intentions and objects assembled together for the warehouse, it was important to blend the occurring relationships harmoniously in order to assemble a sophisticated image. The building's east wing acts as the warehouse's social interface, which is reflected in its friendly geometry. To enable a highly interactive commercial street, a setback on the east side was imposed and a double-story street was formed; people are guided by the yellow markings along the route, which is laid out to highlight the circulation. Big trees are lined up in double rows, outdoor steps are woven with lifted social corners, and diverse street furniture is arranged along the street to trigger comprehensive street movement. Since most of the open spaces within the site are enclosed for the warehouse's functional reasons, we created the roof garden as a gift to the citizens and connected it to street level with the large staircase.

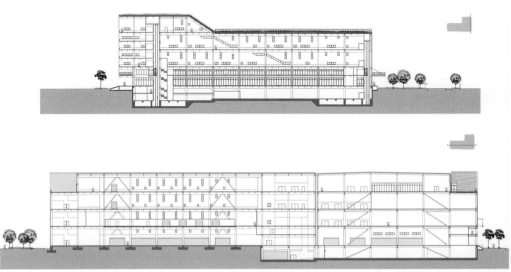

Sections

How do your plans and ideas contribute in deriving a design?

Drawing is the language of architecture and the tool that
conveys ideas and thought. As an architect, you try to
respond to the criteria of a site and the client's proposal by
lots of drawings. Sometimes it works, sometimes it doesn't.
But whatever the outcome, it leaves marks in your brain
and always waits for a second chance to spark. That makes
architecture design an utterly joyful process.

How do you try to understand your clients' intentions?

I.M. Pei said, "The most important ingredient for an architect
to do a good building is to have a good client." That points out
the importance of mutual trust. It is crucial for an architect
to listen and to understand the client's mindset as much
as possible because that is how you distill the core value
of the project. It always begins with a high-quality dialogue
between architects and clients. In this project, we knew that
the client expected more than a massive box and they hoped
to showcase their bold, creative spirit. That established the
common ground for us to grow a strong mutual trust.

How do you incorporate your client's proposals into your design schemes?

We are lucky to have good dialogue with our clients and we notice that the more you engage, the better results you get. To fully understand the proposal of the client is the necessary groundwork that allows architects to check whether the initial programming is confident enough. That also provides the opportunity for the architect to reprogram the building to create something in tandem with the client's expectation. We will not propose a one-sided idealistic scheme. Instead, we secure the practical factor as much as we feasibly can to optimize the scheme.

How do you make evaluations and judgments on your own schemes?

It is a daily routine to improve our design in different aspects again and again. To see if there is a better solution is not just the perfectionist's obsession, but the fundamental of a serious profession. As an architect, it is necessary to challenge yourself and encourage the design team to pursue adjustment constantly.

How do you stay curious in complex and disordered situations?

Cities are complicated and organic. That is why we are keen to create opportunities to motivate interactions between people and buildings, and we believe that it is the obligation of an architect to do more. It is like setting up a flexible backdrop for the city and then allowing citizens to "make their own music;" the most brilliant performance always comes from the complexity and diversity of cityscapes.

When designing, not all of an architect's ideas can always be fully realized. Could you share on how to handle such a situation?

We understand that sometimes it is impossible to put everything together all at once. Some expectations might not manifest immediately due to a realistic reason; it just takes time. But that should not be an excuse to give up good ideas.

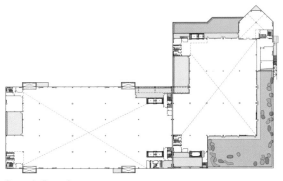

Seventh-floor plan

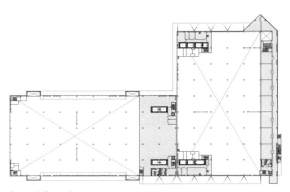

Second-floor plan

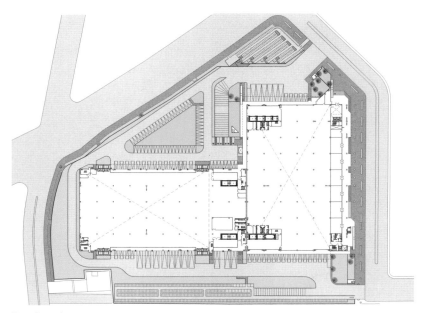

First-floor plan

You still need to push the limit because ultimately, we are suggesting a vision. If you compromise too much, you lose the chance to alter or enhance something.

When you worked on this project, how did you strive to maintain your original idea from beginning to end?

It is important to keep the progress on track, especially when receiving overwhelming information has become normal. It is easy to get lost. Keep your eyes on the focal point and remind the team regularly to exclude excessive, pointless development to ensure effective improvement.

How do you make a comprehensive judgment on a design's progress and optimize the process?

You have to keep the conversation open to take in opinions from your team members. Reviewing the design from different perspectives is definitely significant and it benefits

the project in many ways. When people are passionate about the design, there might be conflicts and debates, but that is, frankly speaking, a necessary and healthy process.

How do you identify critical problems and seek solutions?

The largest issue of the warehouse was how to reduce the visual and operational impact caused by the given volume through smart design strategy. On the one hand, we had to ensure that the warehouse could function at high performance. On the other hand, we also hoped to create a high street. We set the truck path in a one-way system at the opposite corners of the main road, which allowed us to shape a 492-foot-long (150-meter-long) continuous street that is the most important feature of the project.

What role does teamwork play in identifying problems that may have been overlooked?

A positive design process relies on smooth workflow, which means that architects have to take the full responsibility of facilitating seamless, mutual communication. Most importantly, encourage the team members to point out problems and work together when seeking solutions. Stamina and leadership are the key factors to tightening up the whole team, and when you work as a team, you're stepping forward smoothly in confidence.

How do you respond to unexpected problems that occur during the design process?

There are always unexpected "accidents." That is part of the nature of the profession. You are encountering enormous factors and topics and any one of them might be powerful enough to crash the process. It happens all the time. The best way is to take them as a chance to make the project better, even though the process is normally unpleasant. To be optimistic and positive is the best way to respond.

"We encounter many obstacles while designing and we strive to solve them all to the highest and most poetic standards."

Anna Torriani, Lorenzo Pagnamenta

Anna Torriani is a graduate of ETH Zürich and a founding partner of APT Architecture in New York. Torriani pursues her understanding of public space design through the studio's Shaping Public Space (SPS) initiative and public engagement, serving on the Advisory Board for the United Nations Capital Master Plan.

Lorenzo Pagnamenta also graduated from ETH Zürich and is a founding partner and design principal of APT Architecture. Pagnamenta has been researching public space since the beginning of his career through projects and design competitions. He has multidisciplinary experience and is an expert at developing sophisticated design geometry. He leads APT's detail design, sustainable design, and technology aspects. Previously involved in the art world as a painter, he brings an artistic flavor to the studio's projects.

PROJECT NAME---Mariners Harbor Library
LOCATION---New York, United States
COMPLETED---2014
AREA---10,000 square feet (929 square meters)
DESIGN---APT Architecture (Atelier Pagnamenta Torriani)
PHOTOGRAPHY---Albert Vecerka/ Esto, Naho Kubota

Residents of Mariners Harbor—an area with a rich maritime and oystering history—had been asking for a branch of the New York Public Library since the 1930s. The residents' needs included job search services, computer and multimedia access and training, after-school support, gathering spaces, and, of course, traditional book repository and lending facilities.

The new building is located between residential and industrial blocks amid dense foliage. The asymmetrical two-volume form is derived from the biological image of a cracked open oyster shell—the rough exterior of the roof concealing the bright pearls of knowledge within.

The plan maximizes site scale by integrating the library into the neighborhood context, making it accessible and welcoming. The slight shift and bending of the library's volumes creates a hospitable entry and transition into its interior. A larger volume containing reading spaces and a smaller volume containing support functions are organized along an open, glazed central circulation spine linking all services. A community room with audiovisual equipment is accessible at the main entrance, while a terrace in the back garden, with native vegetation and mature trees, is available for patrons' enjoyment.

The metaphor of knowledge as enlightenment is literalized through ample glazing and daylight, providing an adaptable, democratic, and welcoming environment, well suited to this contemporary library's role as a community anchor.

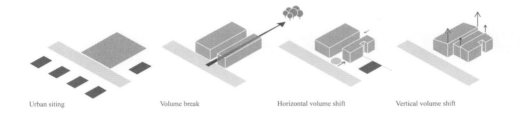

Urban siting   Volume break   Horizontal volume shift   Vertical volume shift

How do you resolve the unfavorable aspects of site conditions?

Every site challenge can be turned into an opportunity. In the case of Mariners Harbor Library, we had a site with street access on the short lot side, which limited the visibility of the building from the road. In addition, the site was surrounded by a large industrial construction outfit to the south and west, a small residential building to the north, and the street to the east. Therefore, we had to solve how to position the new library building and how to create openings for light and air.

How do you put forward solutions comprehensively and objectively without any prejudgments?

There are so many aspects in a project that you need to consider. Trust your instincts. Mariners Harbor Library was a very complex project. The client wanted a one-story building; high visibility from the street with a welcoming entrance;

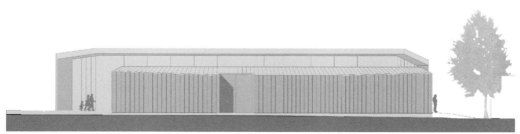

North elevation

East elevation

separate areas for children, young adults, and adults; a
service area; an administration area; and a community
room. At first, we tried to design a mezzanine, but the client
absolutely wanted a one-story space solution.

How do you perceive the abstract architectural space?

We designed the space with the help of 3D software,
developing plans, sections, and elevations throughout. In
every project, we start from the client's desires and program,
while studying in depth the geography, history, and culture of
the site and its people. From these findings and analysis, we
develop various concepts to be reviewed and discussed with
the client. We prepare 3D studies using physical models and
virtual renderings, complemented with plans and sections.

How do you coordinate the relationship between function, space, style, and circulation?

A clear circulation pattern is paramount in the case of a public library. We designed the building approach and the entrance so that patrons feel welcome. Once inside, the glazed spine acts as the main activator where the service station is the main focus. Library reading spaces for children, young adults, and adults are interspersed between the long computer counters and are flooded with diffused natural light. Modern comfortable seats and lounge chairs are available in each reading area.

How do your plans and ideas contribute in deriving a design?

The main concept needs to be verified all the way into construction documents. We started with the idea of the cracked open oyster shell and tried to keep the concept throughout the long review and design process. The client, users, and the many groups that reviewed the project loved the concept. The only problem was how to retain the concept in the actual realization. We were lucky to have the client support the use of a metal envelope, which became a zinc exterior shell.

How do you try to understand your clients' intentions?

In the case of a civic building, we have to first of all understand the program. This library was needed in the neighborhood and the population was mostly young adults and children. The client provided the program and it evolved during the design process. The quantity of shelving diminished and the reading areas were augmented. In addition, the types of reading areas changed over time and access to physical computers became of primary importance for the client.

How do you incorporate your client's proposals into your design schemes?

The second step is translating the needs of the patrons and librarians into a meaningful design. As mentioned previously, we started with an abstract idea, but verified that the required program worked with the "open oyster shell" concept. We knew that the public areas, such as reading and shelving, were much larger than the administrative ones. Therefore, we created a larger volume for the public library functions and a smaller, more discreet area for the support functions.

Section

How do you make evaluations and judgments on your own schemes?

We usually have peer review sessions with our team and outside professionals. The design process for the library was quite long. Since it is a public structure in New York City, it had to undergo many public reviews, not only with the clients, but also with the New York City Design Commission, the local community board, and a designated peer review group. At first, we were not sure what would happen, but actually all these reviews challenged us to improve our design more and more as we went along.

How do you stay curious in complex and disordered situations?

After each review, we would regroup at the studio to plan and debate on how to proceed. We were striving to provide the local community with the best library possible within the given budget, but the task sometimes seemed daunting. We used physical models combined with plans and sections to study the massing, while we prepared renderings to study the interiors. We would sketch changes, verify the constructability with our engineers, and then proceed with implementation.

When designing, not all of an architect's ideas can always be fully realized. Could you share on how to handle such a situation?

For Mariners Harbor, the concept was accepted and welcomed by all—the clients, users, and reviewers— because we had researched in depth the history and geography of the neighborhood. In addition, the "open oyster shell" concept reinforces the neighborhood's identity—an element that is very important in the history and development of New York City. We never considered not being able to implement the concept.

When you worked on this project, how did you strive to maintain your original idea from beginning to end?

We have great experience in designing libraries and we love the typology since it keeps evolving and changing.

Nevertheless, we always checked with our clients about the mundane aspects of the building design, making sure that they understood every aspect of the design and that they felt it was compatible with their vision of a library of the future. We had to revise the internal layouts many times to accommodate directives from the clients.

How do you make a comprehensive judgment on a design's progress and optimize the process?

Good design is a non-linear process. It takes time and you go through all sorts of emotions. A public library is a civic building and, therefore, in New York City, it has to undergo a strict public review process during the design phase and construction preparation. As the architects, we had to follow the process and always be ready to respond to any request, providing all the necessary support to the officials, the public, and our clients.

How do you identify critical problems and seek solutions?

We encounter many obstacles while designing and we strive to solve them all to the highest and most poetic standards. For Mariners Harbor Library, there were many critical junctures and issues, such as the site constraints, natural light and air, and the fact that it was a LEED-rated sustainable building. By shifting the massing of the two volumes, we solved the approach to the building and were able to welcome the visitors who arrive mostly by bus, bicycle, or on foot. For the part on natural light and air, we were able to design a large central glazed roof that provides most of the natural light in the center of the building.

What role does teamwork play in identifying problems that may have been overlooked?

We always work as a team, thus our name Atelier Pagnamenta Torriani, which is abbreviated for ease of pronunciation to APT Architecture. Atelier stands for studio

or group of persons working together. We discuss and research a project for a very long time before starting any design whatsoever. Each partner proposes a concept that is then discussed among the team and we often achieve at least two great concepts for each project. It is the client who chooses. The chosen concept is then tested against the program before going any further with the design.

How do you respond to unexpected problems that occur during the design process?

As we were designing the library, the resident in the house next door to the library became concerned. We knew that the large industrial lot to the south and west was a big contrast to the small house with a garden to the north. We also noticed that there were very large mature trees at the western end of the library lot and in the residential garden. Therefore, we were extremely careful in the massing of the two library volumes, placing the larger library volume against the lot line of the industrial lot and the smaller volume along the residential building. In addition, we left a space along the residential lot and we shifted and bent the smaller volume to acknowledge the residential building and its beautiful trees.

"The beginning of the creative process is the most stimulating part of all the draft stage."

Paolo Balzanelli

Paolo Balzanelli studied architecture at the Polytechnic University of Milan in 1990, graduating with highest honors. He was an assistant professor at the Polytechnic from 1990 to 1995, and a freelance architect in Milan, Strasbourg, and London from 1995 to 2000. Balzanelli established Paolo Balzanelli//Arkispazio in 2000 in Milan. His practice undertakes projects of different architectural scales, including the redevelopment of industrial areas, museum upgrades, and apartment renovations. His works have been featured in prestigious architecture magazines and publications.

PROJECT NAME---Gruppo Cimbali headquarters
LOCATION---Milan, Italy
COMPLETED---2016
AREA---15,069 square feet (1,400 square meters)
DESIGN---Paolo Balzanelli// Arkispazio, Valerio Cometti
PHOTOGRAPHY---Germano Borrelli

Gruppo Cimbali engaged Paolo Balzanelli//Arkispazio for the restoration of two important buildings housing its reception and showroom. The restoration work began with creating a more contemporary space.

The reception building is marked by a new prow-shaped volume that turns to the showroom building. The new volume hosts two new meeting rooms on the first floor and a terrace on the upper level. It also visually absorbs the glass cube of the switchboard. The prow is coated with a pre-oxidized copper skin; the clippings emphasize the vertical rhythm

of the main façade. The material is the same as the existing portal, oxidized with time.

The showroom façade can be seen as a whole, thanks to its curvilinear protrusion. Its simple linear form is emphasized by the pre-oxidized copper-sheet coating, which is also on the facing façade of the reception extension, thereby relating the two renovated buildings to each other.

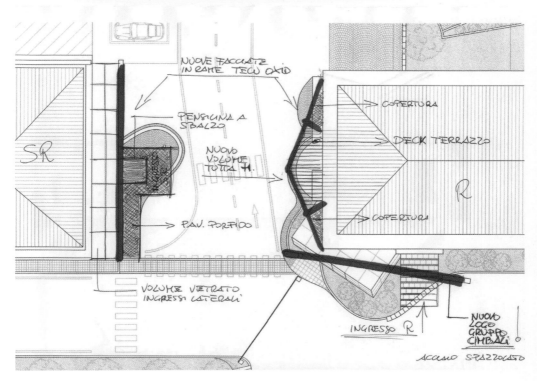

Floor plan

How do you resolve the unfavorable aspects of site conditions?

The site was favorable as it was very large, with easy access from the outside. The biggest problem was having to renovate part of Gruppo Cimbali headquarters without interrupting the company's business. It was possible thanks to a perfect organization of the construction site and a careful division of the workers' routes and the employees' routes. The result was excellent. The company's business was never once interrupted and the renovation was completed without a day of delay.

How do you put forward solutions comprehensively and objectively without any prejudgments?

It is important not to have any prejudgments, leaving the mind free to create something, which with prejudgments would not be possible. It may be important to leave the project for a little time and come back to it with "new eyes." Be open minded; new issues may be noted that were not evident before.

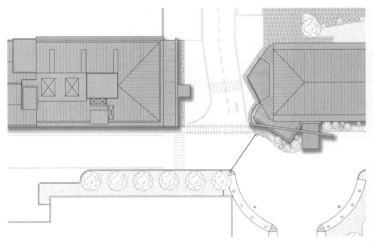

Planimetry

How do you perceive the abstract architectural space?

Very often, I close my eyes and imagine being inside the
space that I am designing and how to move through it. It's
a "dream-like memento," which can bring me new ideas.
For me, architecture is creating a spatial shell within which
people can move. This is the great difference between
architecture and other visual arts.

**How do you coordinate the relationship between function, space, style,
and circulation?**

These are fundamental elements to be taken into
consideration in all projects. I did not change my working
methodology for this project. My concept of style is the
working methodology and not something that has to do with
morphology. And when you talk of shape and function, I can
say that I could probably write a whole book on this subject.
Let's try to think of a simple decanter: the function is always
the same, yet there are many completely different shapes
that we refer to in the same way—decanter. However, there
are decanters for spirits—which need to receive and pour
out easily their contents—and then there are decanters for
perfumes, which instead jealously guard their contents and
are completely different in shape.

How do your plans and ideas contribute in deriving a design?

The beginning of the creative process is the most stimulating part of the draft stage. I start to design the first ideas when I am sure I have carefully analyzed the site and the client's requests. You must always think that the first ideas are not necessarily the best. I start with a deep study and interpretation of the morphology of the site and the client's requests. In this project, one of the most fascinating themes was to confront the pre-existing architectures that were built decades earlier and, at the same time, to develop new concepts related to the new needs of the work/office division.

How do you try to understand your clients' intentions?

The client's intentions and requirements are an essential part of the creative process. The constraints that are located on that path must not be seen as a limitations, but as generating principles.

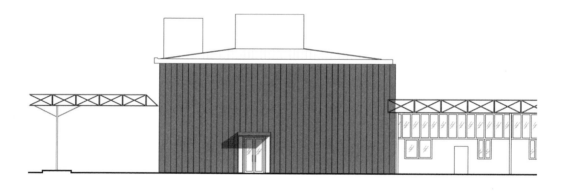

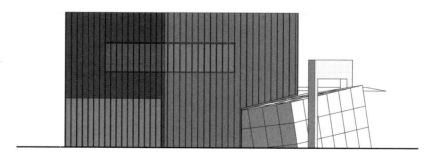

Elevations

For this project, we had to deal with the ideas of the Cimbali family, who have known the world of coffee machines for more than a 100 years, the ideas of their managers, and the ideas that I brought as a designer. It was a very intense and very creative process.

How do you incorporate your client's proposals into your design schemes?

Being a very good architect is not enough to make a good project. The ideas and wishes of the client are a great resource for the designer, especially if the client has, at the same time, experience and a vision that is open to the future. In this particular case, my client represented the most prestigious company in the world of coffee machines, so it was very easy to understand their ideas and interpret them. However, it is very important that an architect does not stop at the first listening of the client's ideas, but makes the effort to go deep and strive to work at its interpretation.

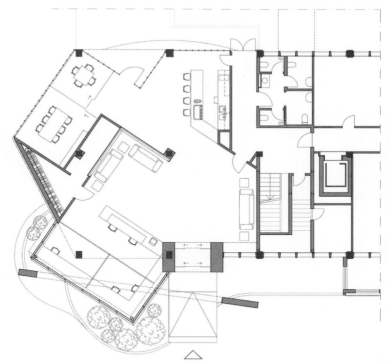

Reception plan

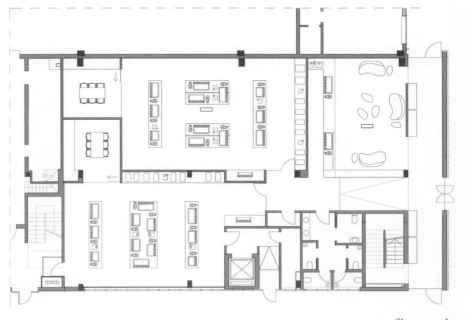

Showroom plan

How do you make evaluations and judgments on your own schemes?

After many years of work, I have gained a working methodology that does not change according to the project: I start from a deep analysis of the site, which can be an external or an internal space, then I analyze the client's requests and ideas and I make an evaluation of the economic budget available. From these three factors and from the reinterpretation, the ideas of the project are born.

What changes from project to project is more precisely the design theme that we have to face and those that we create along the way, which can influence the creation of the architectural form and the choice of materials. For example, in the instance of the Gruppo Cimbali headquarters, I was very struck by the history of this prestigious company, which began more than a 100 years ago building copper boilers. Copper is a material that I love very much and it was also interesting to think about a metaphor of the production of heat. From this theme, was born the spectacular counter

of the lounge bar: 3,000 copper lamellae, which, thanks to backlighting, become incandescent.

How do you stay curious in complex and disordered situations?

Curiosity and the wish to learn and improve every day are basic factors to try to be a better designer and a better person. Without a healthy curiosity, one does not improve in any workplace.

When designing, not all of an architect's ideas can always be fully realized. Could you share on how to handle such a situation?

I do not believe that a creative process cannot be implemented. One must have a consolidated scheme, but it is also ideal to be ready to make changes. For example, the study of the site is the first stage of the creative process, but it must not be done in a schematic and repetitive way. After many revisions and improvements, I believe that any idea will be realized sooner or later.

All ideas for this project were fully developed. After the great success of Mumac Museum that we built for the same client a few years earlier, there was great confidence in us. I still remember the first words of the president of the Cimbali Group, Maurizio Cimbali, who said: "I would like our headquarters to become as beautiful as the Mumac Museum!" At the end of the work, the client congratulated himself on the result achieved and this was one of the greatest satisfactions about this project.

When you worked on this project, how did you strive to maintain your original idea from beginning to end?

> Here, we had conceived a project that started at an architectural scale to arrive at the very finishing details—such as bespoke furnishings. When the project is well-thought-out from the start, it unfolds naturally to the end, like a river that reaches its mouth without encountering obstacles. However, the designer must have the skill to understand if there are any initial errors and know how to correct them without being obstinate with an excess of pride. No doubt, a simple pause in the workflow can go a long way toward helping to understand things. My advice is to deliberately leave the project for a few days; forget it and then look at it with "new eyes" and with a sense of self-criticism. If no defects are found, then you can resume your journey with greater serenity.

How do you make a comprehensive judgment on a design's progress and optimize the process?

> When entering the executive stage of the project, it is very important to optimize the process of work, especially for the variants of the project that, inevitably, will have to be done. Therefore, it is better to be very organized and have a tested way to proceed. Using a parametric drawing software is indispensable to optimize time in tasks that may be monotonous and repetitive.

How do you identify critical problems and seek solutions?

> It can happen very often to have problems during the design process. I look forward to resolving them in a creative way. Sometimes, the problems may improve the project because they make you see things from another point of view.

What role does teamwork play in identifying problems that may have been overlooked?

> We must never forget that architecture is teamwork. We always have to find the suitable technical consultants to

ask the right questions to. That's why I dedicated a lot of time to building my network of consultants and external suppliers, which allows me to easily explore projects of different functional themes, and also to move from small-scale work to large-scale projects. It is no accident that the first monograph of Arkispazio is titled *Thought-out Spaces: 15 Projects from 10 to 1,000,000 Square Meters.*

How do you respond to unexpected problems that occur during the design process?

The main purpose of the project is to anticipate the reality. A good designer must be able to envision the final construct— a few months before what is going to be built and even a few years after construction is completed. However, problems can always happen. Sometimes, a problem may lead to unexpected advantages if you face them without panic and in a creative way. It's not easy and at times, not possible, but sometimes, it can be done.

"In these hectic and overly complicated times we exist in, restraint and reduction serve as a guiding philosophy to achieving subtle beauty."

Fabian Tan

Fabian Tan graduated with Honors from the University of South Australia in 1997 where he received his Bachelor of Architecture. Since then, he has worked at established architectural offices in Kuala Lumpur and Melbourne, handling a wide range of developments that include residential, institutional, commercial, and interior projects for eleven years. During those years, he was also passionately pursuing other forms of expression that resulted in the creation of art pieces, furniture and installations. This experience served as a catalyst to the formation of his own practice, Fabian Tan Architect in 2012. Fabian Tan believes that the essence and consistency of a space is a whole that reflects its constituent parts such as light, material, volume, and relationships.

PROJECT NAME---Bewboc House
LOCATION---Kuala Lumpur,
Malaysia
COMPLETED---2017
AREA---3,700 square feet
(344 square meters)
DESIGN---Fabian Tan Architect
PHOTOGRAPHY---Ceavs Chua

This was a project on a suburban terraced house in Kuala Lumpur, Malaysia, owned by a young family who requested for minimal intervention. The approach was to reimagine a form befitting a corner house and to repurpose the living spaces on the first level.

The new form is simple but bold, contrasting with the existing fabric of tropical suburban homes. From plan view, the living spaces are orientated parallel to the site boundary, resulting in a "break" between the original and new spaces. The triangulated "break" acts as a secured ventilated lightwell, cooling both sides naturally. An arched roof extends outward, creating a

vaulted annex that forms the living spaces. The space appears continuous through the extension of the arch and is exaggerated further through the materiality of the concrete finish from floor to ceiling. The extension is further enhanced by two large doors that open up to the garden. The uninterrupted perspective from inside out immediately connects the interior with nature.

The upper floor sets up a dramatic background with a play of curves and levels. The spaces are layered, creating a hierarchy of space in the layout. The study on the first floor looks out to the living spaces, set next to a step-up platform corner for lounging. Behind this, is a bedroom that overlooks these spaces. The main bedroom connects through a bridge to the outermost floor section of the annex, and much to one's surprise, an open balcony.

To counter the heaviness of the concrete vault, openings were carefully carved out on the upper level. For example, the inverted-arch window at the side of the vault is drawn as a continuous "S" shape when it meets the front arched opening. Walking through the upper levels, this continuity echoes throughout the spaces as lines of openings and arches meet. Consequently, this rhythmic play of lines within a heavy structure lends to a play of light in subtle ways. The experience is reminiscent of a journey through a cave—perhaps to see the light at the end of the tunnel.

Front elevation

Side elevation

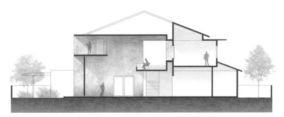

Section

How do you resolve the unfavorable aspects of site conditions?

I don't view unfavourable situations as a negative. They
are part of the site context. I use them as part of a total
creative solution.

How do you put forward solutions comprehensively and objectively without any prejudgments?

Solutions in architectural terms are problem-solving resolutions to the specific questions the site and the client's brief pose. I often view this independently without looking too much into current trends, or looking up other related information on the internet. I believe too many pictures and references can cloud autonomy and creativity. Without these external influences, one can truly focus on the challenges the project itself presents, to be able to resolve design issues objectively.

How do you perceive the abstract architectural space?

For many of my earlier projects and this project, I built physical models to visualise the intended space, accompanied by sketching various options in plans, sections and perspectives. These are not pretty models or sketches meant for publications, rather, they are a process of thorough studies to reflect my thinking and imagination.

How do you coordinate the relationship between function, space, style, and circulation?

Everything that is mentioned is interconnected. I believe that the essence and consistency of a space as a whole is reflected by its constituent parts such as light, material, volume, and relationships. The rule is to simplify the relationships: space, style, and circulation that serve a simple function. In these hectic and overly complicated times we exist in, restraint and reduction serve as a guiding philosophy to achieving subtle beauty.

1 Main bedroom
2 Walk-in wardrobe
3 Main bathroom
4 Stairs
5 Airwell
6 Family room
7 Bedroom
8 Bathroom
9 Lounge
10 Balcony

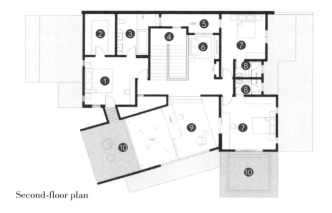

Second-floor plan

1 Living room
2 Dining room
3 Hallway
4 Foyer
5 Car porch
6 Study/studio
7 Storeroom
8 Air well
9 Powder room
10 Guest bedroom
11 Guest bathroom
12 Utility room
13 Laundry
14 Dry kitchen
15 Wet kitchen
16 Patio

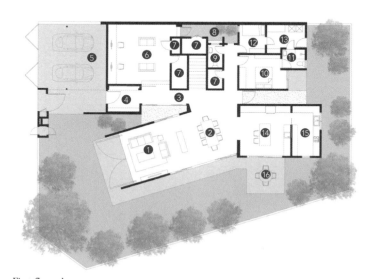

First-floor plan

How do your plans and ideas contribute in deriving a design?

In Bewboc House, the plan and idea began from a skewed boundary. Once the clear idea of aligning the new extension with the boundary was formed, this guided the design of a bold form that breaks from its context, but which still sits naturally among it all.

How do you try to understand your clients' intentions?

Through open communication. These days, most clients are very aware and inundated with information from the internet and their family and friends. For Bewboc House, we were very fortunate to have clients who had very simple wants and who allowed us to create such a bold form. It is central in housing projects that the space designed is comfortable to live in, and that was a priority and assurance we provided to them.

How do you incorporate your client's proposals into your design schemes?

The clients had a straight-forward brief: provide improved living spaces. It was then up to us to follow that brief, but at the same time, negotiate and elevate spatial experiences.

How do you make evaluations and judgments on your own schemes?

I am always refining the design at every stage of the project, even when it is being constructed on-site. I try to trust my gut instinct and am always open to modifying, tinkering with, adjusting, and changing. In this project, many changes were made during construction itself, on-site. This can only be done when you step back from your drawings and feel the space in reality. It was also important to question my previous decisions and keep challenging the details and drawings already done to "check and balance:" Was it still consistent with the initial ideas and concept? Did it strengthen the idea? And to have the bravery to scrap it off, if the answer to the questions are no.

How do you stay curious in complex and disordered situations?

These days, it is a very thin line between being curious and experimental as references are abundant; I try to be introspective of my beliefs and ideas. So maybe, not browsing online too much actually makes me more curious about things. I try to understand all given circumstances deeply without being clouded by internet influences or "added" complexities contributed by other people's opinions, or even online chatter. That way, I can learn about the true fundamentals of the client's needs and the project requirements, and maintain that level of curiosity and learning throughout, regardless of how "disordered" a situation may present itself. For Bewboc House, the vision of the form was clear, and no matter how complex any problem presented itself, it was always about returning to the core of what that original idea was in order to solve the problem.

When designing, not all of an architect's ideas can always be fully realized. Could you share on how to handle such a situation?

I think the idea is not to have too many ideas. Architects always start out with many ideas, but only the most important and relevant one should stay till the end. Going through the process of filtering ideas is a crucial and necessary one and it hones the architect's ability to be more precise. Any "unrealized" ideas become tools to make me sharper in my next project.

When you worked on this project, how did you strive to maintain your original idea from beginning to end?

I believe, sticking to the original idea requires asking yourself good questions throughout the project, because a good question is just as important as a good answer. When working on Bewboc House, I consistently asked myself questions like, "Is this consistent with my idea?" or "Does this new detail resonate with the original idea?" There are times where questions like, "Does this look cool?" or "Is this too simple?" do crop up in my mind, but I always remind

myself that when the question is not correct, the answer is irrelevant. This is a great and important skill to have in navigating the idea and not deviating from the vision and design concept of the project.

How do you make a comprehensive judgment on a design's progress and optimize the process?

A project timeline is often planned out at the beginning of the project, however, like all things in life, it does not always go according to plan. Even with Bewboc House, the design progress met with unexpectant disruptions and I had to simply

take the problems in stride and bite the bullet and just resolve them as best I could. It's important to keep in mind that design progress is not a straight route and being flexible in situations helps optimize the process rather than lengthen it.

How do you identify critical problems and seek solutions?

Often, when critical problems present themselves, they are easily identifiable because they threaten the progress of the project. At this point, there can only be two choices: give up trying or persevere and find a solution. In this project, I chose to put myself in other people's shoes to understand the problem; this meant, oftentimes, stepping out of the role of being just a designer/architect to actively being the person that helps to seek out and negotiate a resolution.

What role does teamwork play in identifying problems that may have been overlooked?

Teamwork is very important in the realization of a successful project. I think good clear communication and integrity is also very important; everything goes toward creating a scenario where everyone has a specific role to play in the building.

How do you respond to unexpected problems that occur during the design process?

Keep an open mind, but never lose sight of the original ideas. Expect the unexpected, rather than stay rigid within a fixed mindset. When we reach a design idea, we have to convince our clients and team to be on board with it. Problems occur when we do not expect that there would be resistance and challenges to our ideas. More often than not, with this project, others would question why I did not choose a conventional way forward. I had to keep reminding myself to be flexible with people and situations, but still maintain believe in my ideas and processes. Not all problems are always architecturally related, so maintaining an open mind with regards to dealing with all relationships formed in the process proved to be very crucial in mitigating unexpected problems.